HOLY CUNT

The Alchemy of Tantra, Relationships and Travel

A Journey into the Divine Feminine

Edited by Karoline Falk and Christy Gibbs

Illustration by Bec Wallis

Cover design by Nic Warner

AYA COHAM

This is the first edition published in the United Kingdom, December 2020 by Aya Coham, printed in the UK by HSP Milners, Ironworks Rd, Barrow-in-Furness LA14 2PG

ISBN: 978-1-8383384-0-4

www.ayacoham.com

Contents

To everyone who dares to venture beyond comfortable,
to be honest and true no matter what
– you are my tribe!

Prelude

When I met Ella, she had escaped a bad tantra retreat the night before. She looked like a forest fairy with her red curly hair, full lips, big green eyes. The little heart tattoo on her breastbone reached out to me flirtatiously. She stared a lot, her eyes filled with fear, drifting with thoughts. Vulnerable and visibly shaken, she'd left her tantra retreat in the middle of the night – had climbed through a fence while chased by barking dogs and a horny man who was supposed to be her partner for the night. She didn't choose him; they were assigned to explore pleasure and enter infinity together. Wow. Pretty intense. In my imagination, he was chasing her completely naked with a raging hard-on. I could almost see the moon illuminating his thinly-haired chest, the mad lust in his eyes. He would be reaching out with his skinny arms as he ran on his long, spindly legs. Even though he was running barefoot, nothing would stop him in his chase for enlightenment – not in a tantric meeting with this gift of the universe.

What a terrible use of my imagination. Disgusted with myself, I look at Ella again. She made it. She's resting now, sunbathing, sipping a smoothie, taking time to feel safe again. This is how I met her; wobbly, unwell, recovering from a forced spiritual near-miss, surrounded by people with crazy stories of their own unique dark night of the soul. These always seem to go hand in hand with spiritual awakenings and breakthroughs.

We're all sitting under a straw roof on the beach, protected from the blazing Indian sun – a bunch of strangers who've only just met, lying comfortably on beach beds, connected and brought closer together by the exotic customs of this country. Everything in India is just so different that you instantly relax when you see the familiarity of a fellow European. The Arabic sea reflects the light from the sky, and I feel grateful to the wind for bringing much-needed relief from the hot temperatures. Next to me is Tony, one of the best tradesmen back in Cornwall – or so says Greg, his companion. Tony is telling us his story:

"Out of nowhere, my Kundalini suddenly awakened. It gave me so much pleasure I couldn't believe it, but it also scared the shit out of me. It released so much darkness, fuck, it was really hard! Most of the time I just stayed in my flat, not knowing what the fuck was going on. And I had this thing about skulls, man, it was like nothing else! I just loved the shapes of the skulls!"

His obsessive thirst for skulls was frightening his

friends and elderly mother. Every time he asked whether he could have her skull after she died, she would say, "Of course, son." She pulled through. His madness passed.

Now he's telling us more details about Shiva, pranayama, and other things he has personal experience of, and as he talks, I drift away, imagining what his mother must have been thinking back then. Wow. I look at him again: shaved suntanned head, strong arms, tattoos. He's a big guy. He has this look about him that tells me he doesn't shy away from fighting. It must have been scary to witness his madness. I'm glad he's well and with us, really enjoying the freshness of his stories – lots of swear words, humor, and the madness and terror of true spiritual awakening.

When you go to Goa or any other place that attracts people on their journey for truth, love, and freedom, you get to hear a lot of stories. And I love to hear them. I have a special section in my brain for safekeeping them. I'm a bit of a storyteller myself. This is my story.

Part One

'For authentic transformation is not a matter of belief,
but of the death of the believer;
[...] not a matter of finding solace,
but of finding infinity on the other side of death.
The self is not made content;
the self is made toast.'

Ken Wilber

Ash

Ash is a guy I share an office with. Us two and eleven others are crammed into a tiny little space in a listed building in the city center. We're supposed to run a zero-paper office, but I just love scribbling in my diary, and people use workbooks and other paper tools for their projects, so zero paper my ass. I really like this office. The walls are dry-wipe, so we can use them for giant mind maps. Lots of semi-professional conversations and bad jokes go on around us all the time, and the girl who was bringing donuts is gone now, thank God.

I just couldn't stay away from those donuts – I swear, they were calling my name every time I walked by, enticing me with the promise of sweet fulfillment in my mouth, stories of feeling so deliciously content. I ate them. And they delivered all the pleasure they whispered about. But only for a moment. The minute the donut was gone, leaving guilty grease marks on my fingers, I was full of regret for the intake of sugar and for having a weak and addictive personality. There's no winning here. You don't take the donut, you keep dreaming about it; you take it, you feel bad about it. And you make a promise to yourself: *"Tomorrow I'll be stronger, yeah, tomorrow I'll ignore them. I won't allow them to have power over me!"*And another fail. So you see, it really is good that she's no longer in this office. Bless her, I hope she found a job where people don't care about healthy food.

Ash is not in my team, but I connect with him. We both cycle to work and live in one neighborhood. On those rare occasions when he's not doing overtime, I'm not in a meeting, and we both finish at the same time, we share our journey home. We like to talk so much that soon we decide to walk, pushing our bikes alongside, just to have a little more time. We talk meditation, spirituality, the meaning of life… we both have a strong commitment to being of service to people.

Ash is tall, with a piercing gaze and chaotic hair, and I just love his laughter. He's smart, passionate, caring, and has an amazingly good heart. It took me six months to develop a crush on him. When I did, I was always on the lookout – is he around? He's on the phone, gosh, he's got such a lovely voice, so warm. Every time I heard him, I was instantly aroused. Every time he looked at me, I was instantly aroused. Every time he'd say, "Hiya, Aya," it was so hard to keep professional! I was almost constantly feeling tickled and sparklingly blissed out. You can imagine just how challenging it was to focus on work that way. It was like having a teenage brain again – nothing else was important anymore. I was half-enjoying it and half-annoyed with myself, as I was barely reaching deadlines and my key performance indicators. And back then, I was seriously interested in building my career. Luckily, it didn't last too long. Ash has a girlfriend and a baby. I can't break up his lovely family. So I do nothing. Just allow myself to feel the intense feelings, but never act upon them. Wow, I didn't even know how *Dzogchen*[1] I was. And I felt so alive. Masturbated quite a lot to release the massive pressure – you know, every little help…

So I enjoyed this crush, this crazy, impossible, amazing thing that was pulling and pushing my mind and body. It brought such an intense spice to my life. There were few moments when I thought perhaps the feelings were mutual, because the space between us was supercharged with excitement, and sometimes we had those awkward moments when you're just frozen, because the thing you really want to do, you just can't. Like touch him

---

1 Dzogchen (rdzogs-chen, lit., 'great perfection') is a teaching of the Nyingma school in Tibetan Buddhism. It is the natural, primordial state and acts as a body of teachings and meditation practices aimed at realizing that condition. The tradition of Dzogchen was brought to Tibet in the eighth century by Padmasambhava and Vimilamitra; in the 14th century it was synthesized by Longchenpa into a unified system. The condensation of this system by Jigme Lingpa (1730–98) remains an authoritative expression of the great perfection tradition up to the present day.

gently on his jawbone or blow a gentle stream of air to that space around his ear… and you're mesmerized by the desire but immobilized because you're not giving yourself permission to do anything with it, and something inside you decides that, if you can't do that, then you won't do anything at all, so you just stand there like an idiot. And then you notice he's doing the same thing, which gives you just enough perspective to move on from this insane moment. Yes, it definitely felt like embodying a teenager again – like pure magic, butterflies in my stomach. What wasn't to like?

I'll never know if the feelings were mutual. Even if he felt the same about me, he likewise never acted upon his feelings – he chose his family, and I loved him all the more for it.

A few months later, this wave of feelings hit the shore and disappeared in the sand. My relationship with him was fully transformed. Sexual intensity waned, but my heart remained fully open. I began to explore sexual energy applied outside of sex. Sexual energy in friendship, workplace, and creativity. This was completely new territory for me, and I was often caught flirting. Friends had a really good time taking the piss out of me, but I didn't mind, I was on a mission. Anyway, this was when Ash told me about ayahuasca.

"What?"

"Ayahuasca."

"Never heard of it."

"That's funny, because people call it *Aya*, you know, your name?"

"Ah, okay. Tell me about it, then."

In my little bubble, Ash was an expert in psychedelics. He wrote his master's thesis on altered states of consciousness, read books, attended seminars… he knew stuff I never knew existed. He had my undivided attention. But there was one problem: there was no shaman in his story. No feathers, no living breathing link to Native Americans. No icaro. No jungle. What kind of fake gathering was he inviting me to?

Given the nature of our relationship, I trust Ash completely, and share my doubts with him now. He looks at me, through me, and says:

"Aya? What's with the feathers and shamans? Are you a little narrow-minded with your spirituality?"

And that does it. He touches something deep inside me. He challenges my identity:

I am Aya and I am open and flexible. I love diversity and freedom. Oh, but I'm totally extreme when it comes to spirituality – it has to have feathers and shamans, otherwise it's not real, sorry.

No, no, no. That's not right. I know, it was because shamans and feathers and tipis formed a *Maloca*; a home for my spiritual practice, a bridge for reaching the great beyond. And I saw how I'd become dependent on that bridge for my spiritual practice. But that was foolish of me. Native Americans don't need props to connect with Spirit, they are always connected. So I must be also… it's just that I'm just not that advanced. I'm a toddler crawling about in this dimension. Okay, time to let go a little and risk a few steps.

Moments like this – and I mean moments of outgrowing limiting assumptions and worldviews – are only possible when I risk being true and open with myself and with others. I expressed myself freely with Ash and he responded to me in a similar way; challenging me openly to my face. And then, *bang,* suddenly I see my limiting assumptions clearly. A moment ago, I wasn't even aware that I was discriminating against other spiritual practices. But it was part of my identity. The temporary constellation of ideas that made Aya. A structure of characteristics I chose to adopt along the way. Some are very obvious to me – I am a caring, mindful, feminine being who's proud to have a deep insight into what's what of the human experience. A clarity of mind, a drive for passionately relating with others, creative… you get the drift. Other characteristics are hidden, more part of the unconscious, like the fear that I'm not whole without a partner, or that spiritual practice requires a shaman.

Really, the only chance we have with this grid of rules that builds our identity is a sense of humor. The more we can laugh at ourselves, the looser the structure of the characteristics, thus the more freedom we have. Freedom to choose what to do next. Freedom to express ourselves in any situation – the only true freedom available to us. It's a powerful thing.

Ash has invited me to truly own my spirituality, to be free from any spiritual belief system, including the one that makes the most sense to me at the moment – feathers and shamans.

Okay then!

We choose a date and make arrangements. We have five months to get ready for a ceremony of a lifetime.

Are you a medicine plant person? I'm telling you, they're no joke. It's the second day of the ayahuasca retreat and I'm sweating; the 2.5 million eccrine glands spread throughout my skin are oozing liquid through my pores and making my clothes wet. My heartbeat is fast and irregular, like a horse that saw a snake and took off for his life. My thoughts are scattered – I'm not even sure what I'm thinking about, can't catch any of them before they change into something else. I've been in a state of mild panic for half a day now. I'm exhausted, but the adrenaline keeps me going. I can't find a place to rest, I'm thinking of running away from here. After the first ceremony last night, I realized there was no way of outsmarting ayahuasca. No way to wiggle or navigate my way through it with positive attitudes and good thoughts.

You know, like when you take LSD and you get in a nice mood with nice thoughts and nice people around… a recipe for a nice trip. Not here, no way. This plant takes you completely and fully, grabs you by your ankles, guts, hair, whatever else – there's no escaping it. I was petrified. The first night wasn't bad, but somehow, I thought maybe it was beginner's luck. I witnessed the pain and suffering of all the people around me, purging and releasing darkness. I was scared shitless. I was imagining dark twisted demons waiting for me there.

I tried to calm myself down; I was breathing, stretching, walking, sitting in meditation… nothing worked. Actually, the anxiety grew like a gigantic air balloon, ready to take off. I was so lost. I was planning my escape plan, but deep in my heart, I knew I would never dare to leave this space, alone and in this vulnerable state.

Suddenly, I found myself standing in front of Anarim, the medicine man. He was a tall, big man, like a mountain, and just as grounded, calm and still. He looked deeply into my eyes, through me, and he smiled. He asked how I was, and I burst into tears. He just hugged me and allowed me to cry until I had no tears left in me. When I was ready, I took myself out of his hug, and he nodded and said:

"Yes, it's pretty scary."

He said nothing more. I said nothing either, just nodded. What could I say? This was the essence – he named it perfectly, acknowledged it. Somehow, he found a way to meet me there, compassionately, with no wasting of words. Completely and utterly, with his undivided attention and presence. And it helped. It gave me just enough space for a proper breath. I was standing on the ground again.

Now, there are still a few hours to go before the second ceremony. I'm afraid that if I allow my mind to wander aimlessly, I'll end up in the same space of fear and despair. I need to do something, focus my attention, find a way to self-discipline...

I get my drum out of the boot of my car, find an empty room in the house. Sit down on a cushion. Close my eyes. Connect with the hide, with the beater. Just breathing in silence for a while, holding my drum close to my ears. A potential of rhythm. A possibility of sound. Silence. I'm well aware of the twenty other people occupying this big house at this moment, and feel acutely aware of the disturbance I would make.

Here is an edge. Do I sit silently, or do I make a sound? Maybe I wait it out. Distract myself with a conversation with someone. Pass my time somehow before embracing my death sentence tonight.

Deep in my belly, I know.

No. This is why I came here. I want to face my fear. I want to understand what's lurking deep in the shadows. I came here because I'm longing for a breakthrough. This is it. I'm breaking through the self-constraining rules I made for my-

self.

So I make a first bang. Pause. Another one. Nobody is shushing me, nobody is coming to punish me for the violation of a rule that's only in my mind. So I continue. Shy at first. Chaotically. Then I find a rhythm. It's so familiar. *Ba-ba-dam-ta-ba-dam.* Effortlessly stable, calm. I feel an invitation to settle in those spaces between the beats. Then the rhythm changes a little, and then comes the voice to join it, deep from the belly. I feel the resonance of the vibrations in my chest. Soon I'm drumming and singing like there's no tomorrow, and I'm not even sure when everything else disappeared. There are no walls or floor around me, no trees or sky outside – just the intense current of the vibrations. The darkness behind my closed eyelids is vast. I am no longer local. I am expanding and contracting in fractal-like movements, filling all consciousness. There are no visions, just a sensation of being spread across everything there is with the substance of myself. Ever-unfolding movement in every direction.

Slowly, the vibrational infinity seizes, and everything turns into silence. My breath. I wonder what I would see if I open my eyes. A few more breaths. I allow the light in and see a lot of people sitting in lotus position in front of me on the carpet, palms up in receiving mudra. Wow. Okay. Anxiety is way gone. Shyness is back in. But there's also a deep connection with myself and everything around me. I am ready to meet ayahuasca and welcome whatever's going to come tonight.

A couple of hours later, Anarim finds me sitting under an old ash tree just outside the yurt. It's cold and refreshing. My body is softly wrapped in warm blankets and I'm enjoying the cool wind on my face. He asks me if I'd like to share the medicine songs tonight at the ceremony that I learned from the Native Americans. I'm shocked. My ego is jumping up and down, throwing confetti and blowing the trumpets. Yes! She is already standing on the podium, wearing her best clothes, receiving the framed certificate for being the real-deal-singing-shaman as thousands of people in the audience cheer for the well-deserved appreciation of my lifelong efforts to be genuinely beautiful and pure. But before she makes her thank you speech, I manage to silence her. Gosh. I feel awkward and shy, and ashamed of my ego.

Right. To sing at the ceremony tonight?

Anarim is waiting patiently for my response.

My intention for coming here was to learn more about the magic of sound healing. I was asking the medicine to show me the mysterious way it works. And now I have an opportunity to sing with her. Really?

I feel so grateful and honored and shocked. I didn't see it coming. I'm not sure I can do it, though. And I share my concerns with the Medicine Man. He finds the words to reassure me and I agree, feeling so very grateful for the opportunity to experience my voice in that space. In abandonment and surrender.

Singing with the medicine in my system showed me everything I was hoping to learn about sound healing, and so much more. A couple of years later I would still be unpicking the complexity of my experience and visions. My voice and drum created a powerful vortex in the yurt. Energy circled around and up. This current of energy had the potential to carry anything people wanted: prayers, healing of wounds, visions. I know now just how important intent is. It has to be pure and absolute. It is the key element in the process. This experience was such a bountiful gift. It kickstarted a deep experiential exploration of sound and intent. It opened a door in my cognitive mind for possibilities that were unavailable to me up until that point. I also understood that sound was my medicine and I need to share it with others. This is my gift. One of them.

I was on my fourth song when I realized how powerful this was, and I got excited about it. I started thinking about it and my mind wandered off the track, I was no longer focused on drumming and singing. Once I realized I was focusing on the excitement of the experience rather than purely on being in the moment, I stopped. Anarim was right there for me and swiftly took over. The ceremony continued naturally. No confetti. No certificate. Boy, I was so pleased with myself that I stopped right there, so happy that I didn't fall prey to my ego trap. I truly am an experienced ego stalker. To be honest with you, I don't think ego ever stops trying. It's not a *one-battle-and-you-can-rest-now* kind of thing. You've got to have your eyes in the back of your head to stay aware of the stubborn fucker. Or better yet, keep surrendering, accepting, and having compassion for this part of yourself, knowing that the ruling time of individual ego is coming to an end.

Ego and the Critic. Two buddies. What a nightmare. I have plenty of stories with these two villains. Let me tell you a story of dream work that I had been doing a few years back.

For one year, I was training myself in lucid dreaming. I had read a few books about the amazing potential of being awake while dreaming and I wanted this. The shamanic possibilities of this practice were flirting with me, whispering of unimaginable feasts I would devour in its company. I was too shy to admit it, because I like to be a humble kind of person in the eyes of others, but in secrecy, I was aiming high. Imagine yourself being able to travel to real places in real time, checking things out, learning languages... did you know that a short meditation while dreaming reaches far deeper than all waking meditations you could possibly do in a lifetime? I must admit, I was already feeling happy imagining the outcomes I would achieve, and I was nowhere close to lucidity. But I didn't allow that brutal fact to cool me down, not at all. I became a committed novice. Every night, just before going to sleep, I focused my intention on my goal: to see my hand in my dream.

I'll see my hand, I'll see my hand, I'll see my hand…

And every morning I would painfully acknowledge that I hadn't. Again. But I kept going strong. Until after a year, I could! Can you believe it? And it was nothing like what I'd expected...

I am in a dark alley with three men. They have dark intentions and I'm afraid of them, trying to work out my escape, what to do next. I look down and see my arm first, then my hand. I raise it to my face and smile wildly. I know it's a dream,

I'm dreaming!

The same kind of awareness that's normally present in the day knows I'm sleeping and that this is my dream.

How amazing!

I look at the guys, wave at them, and shout happily:

"I see my hand! I see my hand! I see my hand!"

In the next moment, the three men are gone, dissolved into thin air, and I'm alone in the dark alley. And my daily awareness is thinking:

Okay, so I'm dreaming… what shall I do? What shall I do? Oh my God, oh my God, this is so exciting!

But I'm a little puzzled. I really don't know what to do. I feel like I have a lot of choices, but that they're all in the dark, unavailable. For a moment I just stand there, indecisive, looking into the darkness in front of me. Confused and excited. And then an idea: I want to fly.

Yeah, this is going to be fun! I'm dreaming and I'm going to fly!

And then I woke up. My eyes wide open, fresh and bright. I looked around the room: the ridiculous pink armchair gifted to me by my sister, beige wallpaper – boring standard neutral finish in a rented accommodation in South London.

I had a moment of triumph.

Ha! All those nights of trying and finally, I did it!

But it wasn't the kind of magnificence I'd imagined. The good feelings didn't last long enough to make me smile. Instead, the totality of my existence was filled with bitter disappointment. One year of setting intention for this?

This is it?

My inner critic was armed, safety off, and she was ready for slaughter.

You're such a loser! One year of setting intention and you can't even be calm and still when it happens, you just got over-excited like a baby. What an idiot, you never even planned for what you'd do when you saw your hand. You're a waste of time and space – you got this gift and you blew it.

You know, inner critics are the toughest. You can count on them to mentally punish you like no one else. She was taking her time to convince me of all the reasons why I was worthless. She was indulging in her cruelty. She didn't even have to try hard. With a precision of a landmine designer, she was navigating the land of my deepest fears and was threatening to unearth them, to reveal the ugliness of an idiot, a loser, a naive little girl who didn't know a thing about life – just another wannabe, a preposterous imitation. It crushed me so bad. I felt nailed to the bottom of the sea, unable to move, to breathe. No chance for rescue. So I did what people usually do in similar circumstances. I quit and completely lost interest in lucid dreaming.

But I didn't let my inner critic destroy me completely. My ongoing practice at the time was about developing self-compassion and self-love. It's outrageous that we actually need to train ourselves and cultivate it, that it doesn't come naturally to us.

So as I'm practicing love and compassion for myself, I just assume that for some reason, this experience with lucid dreaming was an important part of my journey – just not something I understand fully yet. I can't see how it's of benefit to me yet, but I will one day. And really, if I look at the facts, the whole thing is an achievement; I showed endurance trying for one year with no results, and I reached my goal precisely: I went beyond the boundary of un-self-awareness while dreaming. That's amazing.

Of course, at the same time, it's not that significant. Just a drop in the ocean of awareness. But it's a good step on my journey. I see that I can dream the impossible. I can trust myself to keep going when I choose what I want. How about that. But what do I want?

Do you know what you want?

The Witch

I had this beautiful moment with one of my trees this morning. Standing in the grove, the early sun made its way through the foliage silently, shining bright on the green and yellow leaves.

Birds are singing up above and humans are calling their dogs in the distance. I brought a few seeds and am scattering them around while saying my prayer of gratitude for the abundance of life I get to experience. After giving thanks for everything and everyone in my life, I feel high, my body shaking slightly, my vision a little blurry. I feel a tingling spaciousness in my belly – it tickles me in a way no lover can. And I feel whole and complete. Did you know you can get high on gratitude? Just try it.

I have a sensation of being pulled just below my heart and know that the tree is inviting me to make a wish. Don't ask me how I know. It's like knowing you're hungry or that you need to pee. You just know.

Tears of joy come to my eyes. Nature has such a capacity to hold and support us. All we need to do is to let it in. It's such a powerful, positive thing. It's the ultimate mother archetype. Giving, giving, giving, and then giving some more. I'm so moved. I can't think of anything I want. In this moment, I feel so connected to myself. There's a sensation of completeness – I have no burning needs that I can't meet myself or slowly work toward.

I take my time for reflection. I recollect the times I spent in the company of trees. They mean so much to me. They share their calm, soothing presence with so much dignity, so subtly. The last tree I spoke to witnessed a very important rite of passage for me. It was an oak tree, growing in an old cemetery in East Bristol, with a round patch of grass around it and a bit of pavement. This round pavement isn't connected to any other path there – it just takes you round and round the tree. It's dark now. The chapel is to the north. I sit facing south with my back against the tree. Gravestones are scattered around chaotically. Not a single human being in sight. The sounds of the city flow into the space as if reassuring me that the world is still spinning and everything is as usual. Good. I'm going into a trance.

I take a moment to connect, to feel my roots intertwining with the tree's. I know how deep they go and how deliciously moist the soil is. I open up through the top of my head, merging with the crown of the tree, feeling the wind and the moon caressing us both gently. I open my heart to connect with the essence of the tree and welcome all the bones of humans and animals that are resting in the soil. So many stories; love, hatred, comedy, drama, jealousy, crimes, heart-warming reunions and forgiveness. I thank them for doing their best. I tell them I bring gifts and scatter lavender flowers around me, for purification and letting go. I surrender more into my experience. I came here to reunite with the Witch. I look up. The sky is clear. I see sprinkles of stars. I open my mouth and start singing the recurring nightmare from my childhood.

When you're dreaming, you don't know it's just a dream. It's so realistic. Your mind makes it so. Even though I've had this dream so many times before, I can't remember it. I just know that She will find me. I don't know what She's going to do with me, but I'm so afraid of her. I'm hiding behind the sofa in the living room. I know my parents can't stop her. They're here, standing by the windows, not moving, not talking. Everything is at a standstill. The Witch is walking just outside the windows. She walks past our house. I find no relief in this though. I know she will find me. Every muscle in my body is tense. I'm crouching down on my heels, holding on to my calves. Holding on to my life. I'm only five or six. The sofa is guarding me. The Witch is back. She opens the door, goes through my parents like they're ghosts. She is coming. She cuts through the room, straight to my hiding place. She is reaching for me, her nails almost dragging across my skin. And I wake up. Sweat on my body. A silent scream in my throat. Except that I don't make a sound, because she might hear me.

Then I realize it was a dream. But that's no solace either. Somehow, she's more than just a dream. She lurks in every shadow, behind the mirrors, under the kitchen sink, between the floorboards. For a moment, I just stare into the darkness of my room, refusing to fall asleep again. But then I always do. She never comes back again the same night. But she is always back.

Until she was gone. At last. After many years of recurring nightmares. Freedom. Or so I thought.

I'm almost forty now. It took me a long time. I whisper my apologies to the starry night. I tell them I didn't understand. But I'm ready now. I've been living with fear my whole life. It never held me back. Rather, it kept me stuck to the archetype of a warrioress. Fearless and strong. Pushy. I was fast, ambitious, driven, and focused. And in this race, I completely disregarded my true self. Because of fear of who I am, of my true power. Fear that if I stop for long enough and listen, I might hear a completely different song of Aya. A song so different from 'normal' that I would be exiled. Feared. Rejected. What an irony. I have been feared and rejected by myself instead.

Various lifetimes. The family scars – my mother's and her mother's and hers before… and so on in all the women from the beginning of humanity. The deep earthy wisdom they carried, I too carry in my bones. Their pain and rejection are at the forefront. It shows in my lifetime too, as patterns and stories that I'm attracted to like a moth to the light of a bulb. They are all inviting me to heal, surrender, let go of them, with love and compassion.

Yes, I am a different person. It all ends with me. I am no longer afraid. I will listen. I will become a dedicated apprentice of Me. I've been procrastinating long enough. I am ready.

Daring to Go Beyond

Ayahuasca was my second medicine plant. She came five years after peyote. All this came to me by surprise, as an invitation from my friend, Slav – a bodybuilder, physio, and massage therapist. His favorite thing in the world is to visit friends unexpectedly, just because he's in the area. I suppose he does it because he can; he commutes on his fast and furious motorbike, massage chair wrapped tightly around the whole structure, flowing freely through the traffic and secured by the muscles of his shoulders, propelled by the mechanical muscles of the bike. A text message read:

"Hiya, are you home? I could pop in 20 minutes."

He came early evening on Thursday. Cup of tea, greetings. He brought a tin of food for my dog, he's so cute. I know he means well. Still, I can't help but wonder:

Does he think I starve Tryton?

Never mind.

He told me he'd been invited to a Native American Church gathering organized by Polish people north of London, and wondered if I'd like to go with him. A gathering in a tipi with a shaman and peyote. My jaw dropped with curiosity and excitement. He was opening a door to a completely new world for me. Tipi, peyote, Polish Native American Church… wow. I really wanted to go, but it sounded like some kind of next-level shamanic shenanigans. How did I know it was safe? Not that I was sure if *safe* was a good word when it comes to journeying beyond the limits of one's mind. Rather, how did I know it was genuine?

I have always been daring. They say that the way you're born contains a complete blueprint for your life, and that's why we can't remember it. All I know is that I came to this earth a month too early and didn't need medical assistance. And that shows through and through. I go where others don't want to. My parents seemed to struggle with me on and off the whole time. At the age of thirteen, we moved to a newly-built estate with more than two thousand families. New school, new peeps. You'd expect a typical teenager to shy away, crawl into a shell and wait it out until it's safe again. Not me, thank you very much – I was actively meeting my peers until I created my new tribe, only to lose it by the age of fifteen in a tragic argument with my best friend, who in a heroic struggle turned everyone against me, which then resulted in two years of the worst bullying in the history of that community. Maybe it would've been better to have waited it out after all. But then I wouldn't have received the teachings that came with it.

I really wanted to experience the Native American Church, but I had my doubts. I decided to call the organizer of the gathering and follow my gut instinct. I figured that even though my eyes often got caught by shiny things and my mind lost in pretty stories, my guts never lied.

Olympia's voice was warm, caring, and calm. She wasn't trying to push any agenda or to encourage me to come. That was it – I was in! Of course, I think I was actually *in* the moment Slav mentioned it, I mean, come on, anything that comes out of this kind, tall, unshaven man with muscles so big it's unreal, I would take in like a sweet little chocolate truffle.

Two days later I was sitting in a large tipi with a bunch of strangers. Slav didn't come, he'd had a last-minute thing, so I was there by myself. So many people, everyone looking both relaxed and alert, smiling.

We're sitting hip to hip in two rings around the fire. The shaman is wearing feathers and has a serious expression. I'm not the only newbie, which for some reason reassures me. The shaman gives a good introduction, his voice steady and confident. In the pauses between his words, I hear more reassurance. I also feel that all this information is based on the roots and foundations his people have been cultivating for hundreds and thousands of years. His words and melody of his speech rest comfortably on this foundation. I'm hearing lots of rules:

"Sit straight, always in contact with fire. No closing eyes, no drifting away in colorful visions; we are here together until sunrise. Nobody leaves, nobody walks between fire and shaman, and only walk clockwise if you absolutely have to go out for a moment. Only leave between prayers, never during one, never during medicine round…"

The list is long, but I actually like it. Strangely enough, all this feels like home. As the night progresses outside the tipi, I keep still, sitting on the ground, enjoying the warmth of the fire and the melodies of medicine songs. I'm curious and eager, I keep taking everything in, and… nothing happens. No thunderbolt, no visions, no breakthroughs, no purging, no healing.

Just before sunrise, four women bring in water and fresh, raw food. This is a ceremony on its own. One of the women is invited to sit opposite the shaman, her back to the entrance. She's given sacred tobacco and some time to talk. I have goosebumps hearing her speech of gratitude, love, the feminine energy of Mother Earth providing us with everything we need and asking for nothing in return. There's a beautiful flow to her words – a current of kindness caressing the air around the fire. It affects my heart, my ears, my eyes. The woman becomes an embodied locality for the divine feminine. She's so smooth, sweet, and nurturing just by being here. In the way she sits and looks around at everyone, we instantly receive the greatest gift a mother can give: a deeply caring presence. My gaze locks with hers for one moment and I know that I am wanted here, I am needed. I am welcomed to show myself fully, to unravel my gifts and share them abundantly. I have tears in my eyes. I'm very grateful for the invitation, but I'm not sure I can do it. *It's okay*, her eyes say. Then she changes her tone a little and we get to see other aspects of the divine feminine. She becomes demanding – she wants us to stand up and act in the world like it's our home. She does it in a very empowering way, like a great enchantress. The more I listen, the more I grow in understanding of the little ways in which I can improve the environment and how I can contribute to building a loving family that we have the potential to become, as a human species on this planet. It becomes part of my DNA. It's so simple. It doesn't have to be big, really. I don't have to change the world single-handedly. I get it. I become so eager to meet her desires. I want this too. For myself, for my family, for my friends. How amazing would it be to live in a world that's just a gigantic supportive network of creatures, humans, plants, rocks, clouds, and everything else? One that you love dearly and that loves you and has your back, always? This vision might be far off, but it's certainly worth heading toward.

She pauses for a moment, the sacred tobacco in her hand. The shaman looks at her and says:

"That's it?"

Giggles around the fire.

"Usually, when a woman starts talking, you just can't find a way to stop her."

She looks up at him, fire in her eyes. Now comes the witch. She gladly accepts the invitation to take up more time, to bring up the concepts that are the most difficult to accept. She shines them brightly, right in our eyes. Tired after the whole night of sitting upright, with pain in my hips and knees, I drift off to second attention, very much awake and aware but not so rigid in making sense of what's what. I see how everyone is trying hard to be a good person. Good in the light of personal values; an unwritten code of conduct dictated by history, ancestors, social norms. I see how it could become a trap, causing people to inhibit and repress their thoughts, feelings, and behaviors. We waste so much energy reining ourselves in. Because we don't own our stories, because we don't own our shit. Because we try hard to be good. Because we're afraid, because we're not. Trying even harder to be good is bound to bring frustration. Annoyance. It creates a ghost energy of violence. It serves as fuel for passive-aggressive behavior. The witch in me opens her eyes. She points her finger at the collective shadow. Murky, sticky, a dark space of unwanted desires, inner conflicts, self-destruction, and so much more. The darkness grows bigger and bigger and I see so much in there. All the details of fear, pain, rage, self-inflicted cruelty; a disgusting fly-strewn field of a human mind. The deep darkness is enveloping me. A moment of panic.

How did I get here? Why am I here?

Because you want to be a healer, she says.

Finally, a big bowl of water goes around the circle. I bring my lips to the rim and tip the bowl up. Water slowly travels through the dry cracks on my tongue. I'm only taking a small sip to make sure others get some too. I lift my tongue and the water touches the roof of my mouth. Wow. The whole cavity of my mouth fills with cold, earthy, life-giving liquid. I feel like I never drank before this moment. Tears of gratitude flow down my cheeks. I feel so much love and so much awe for nature, which continues to nurture us despite our cruelty to it.

It's time to leave the tipi and meet the sun. It feels like being reborn. People around me are all high on love and compassion. Everyone seems so connected with one another and with the nature around us. And I feel so connected, too. I speak with the wind, and it tells me my name is Aya and that I'm doing well. "Keep going," it whispers to me.

And that's how it started (again). So many beginnings, huh? I've come to think that we actually start many times. Every time we dare to stop, we start again. Every time I dare to go beyond my fear, I do something completely outside my comfort zone – I go seeking adventure with an open heart, I discover new worlds that forever change who I am. This night and morning were seemingly uneventful – there was no dramatic happening, no near-death experience. And yet a profound thing has happened; a seed of Native American indigenous spiritual tradition was sowed in my heart, in my mind, and in my way of understanding the world. Many years later, I will run a charity in Bristol where people sit in circles and share stories of darkness, hopes, and dreams with courage, looking deeply within, being together in acceptance, supporting one another. No medicine plants, no feathers, no shamans or songs. A Western, urban tipi in a community center, a library, a cafe… that's just one of the fruits that came from that seed. A seed that grew into a mighty tree, branching out in all directions to include the whole of creation; a seed of spiritual life. What a gift! My family was Catholic, and despite going to church every Sunday, I never made a connection with anything outside of this consensus reality. Even when I sang hallelujah in the choir, even when I gazed at the colorful glasswork in the cathedral rosette window, I felt nothing. I was angry at God for giving me my dull, sour life full of pain and hardship, but I never believed Him to be real anyway. Just a story of a long time ago. A bunch of stories, actually, designed to keep me at bay, in fear of hell. But life seemed like hell already. So I was in spiritual limbo.

The Native American Church gave me a firsthand experience of the realm beyond the material world. That gathering in the tipi ended years of my spiritual poverty. And even though I disregarded some of their rules when developing my own practice, I will be forever grateful to them. I have a deep respect for all the Mexican and American medicine men and women traveling to Europe to share their knowledge. It's a big movement now – just check your local sweat lodge on Facebook, you'll be surprised at what you'll find.

Part Two

"Life path:

#1 Show up

#2 Pay attention

#3 Tell the truth

#4 Stay open to results"

from Rumi's 'One Song'

Let Go & Surrender

We're going up in a lift with Kirt. It's a tiny little space, very futuristic, like from a sci-fi movie. Soft white lighting emanates from the walls, the ceiling, the floor. It feels bright and milky, and surprisingly comfortable. I gaze at his face and find solace. I like his full lips, blue eyes, and long blond hair that's a little burnt from the straightener. He smells of his raspberry lip balm. He flexes his muscles, looking at me provocatively, a playful smile on the corners of his lips. I giggle. I like every bit of his adopted celebrity-style persona. It suits him. We arrive at the top floor, the door opens – and it's all clouds. Everything is white and fluffy. I look around, bewildered. Kirt isn't surprised at all. He walks over to the bar and invites me to follow. There's no bartender, but things are materializing out of nowhere, just as we want them. With a gesture, he invites me to try some local chocolate. It looks like a little fluff of cloud. I put a piece in my mouth and I am dazzled – it tastes like all my favorite chocolates at the same time: cold GU-chocolate cheesecake, the hot melted center of a chocolate pudding, the crispy top of a brownie in the Mokoko Café… this is sensational! I give in to the deliciousness of it. Kirt is smiling so intensely that his eyes are shining. We are no longer in Samsara or Maya. This is paradise. I feel like this is just the beginning, that Kirt has so much more to show me about this place. And now I understand. The heaven we reached is based on the pleasure of having and doing, delightfully fulfilling our sweetest desires. This heaven of having and doing is delightful, but it's not what I want. Not even one bit. What I want is heaven of *being*. Without a sound, I spread my arms, look at him one last time, slowly allow my body to lean backward, and start to fall…

awake. I'm still sitting in meditation. I must have been sitting for a long time. I can't move my legs. I clearly remember sitting for ages, witnessing my mind relentlessly focusing on stuff – latching onto anything just to escape the nothingness as I focused on my breath, the warmth within my blanket, perspiration, stories, more stories… and then I reached a trance. I wasn't asleep and wasn't awake. Thoughts were gone.

It's tricky to stay there. You have to keep relaxing, keep resting as your experience, not get excited about it and judge it. It's so important because the moment you try to frame anything in language, this trance state is gone, and you're back in your ordinary state of the mind. A lot can happen in a state of trance. I mean a lot. A single time spent in trance can change you forever. That's if you don't disregard it as just your imagination. And then it changes everything. At the same time, it changes nothing – you still do the dishes and pay the bills, but it changes how you do it, your relationship with them and with yourself.

I didn't stay in the trance, not this time. Instead, I fell asleep, sitting.

Wow, that's new. I'm really going beyond limits.

My inner critic is fluent in sarcasm.

But the message in that dream is undeniably valuable.

Kirt is a porn producer, tantra practitioner, and guru. He's a real man – one with whom I'm having this amazing, crazy, psychedelic journey. He's a joker and a con man. A giant walking cock who knows no limits. A genius who went through a spiritual by-pass. A funny and arrogant magician who pushed me far into the abyss when I was pursuing the uncovering of the ultimate truth.

I know he's reading this now, somewhere out there. He could be sitting right next to you. I know he's curious about what I will reveal. He's in for a surprise.

The beginning of Aya and Kirt was like honey and lemon on a pancake – sweet and fulfilling, but as soon as any promise of a romantic relationship appeared in the air, everything changed and I was heading into the biggest shitstorm I'd ever experienced, heart-first. Relentlessly and because I loved him so insanely, I kept turning every challenge into golden dust of wisdom. The kind of knowing that only comes through experiencing life at its fullest, when you take risks and go all the way. You get burned, yes, but you stay around the fire and keep working with it, keep learning from it – and then you really get to know it. Not because you're clever, not because you're able to wiggle or navigate your way out, but because you surrender fully, died and are reborn.

When I first saw Kirt, I didn't like him at all. Very pretty, boyish, confident, using his looks to grab attention. He looked like he had thousands of girls in his life.

I showed his photo to my friend and her immediate response was:

"Watch out for this one, he's got chlamydia written all over his face!"

We both burst into giggles. I knew what she meant. I heard it too, a little warning. Just a little whisper echoing:

This guy is dangerous and if you value your comfort, wellbeing, or sanity at all, you'll stay away.

I knew this the minute I saw him. I didn't want to become his next victim, so I chose to ignore him. And to be fair, I came to this retreat for ayahuasca, not romance! I hadn't done this medicine before. I was scared and excited.

The retreat starts like any other retreat I've been to – medicine plants or not. Warm welcomes from the hosts, a mix of apprehension and a sensation of coming home. People smiling shyly. Soon enough we'll all be hugging like koala bears, feeling so much connection. But not yet – now we are all acutely aware of our separation and non-belonging.

I'm summoned to have a chat with my helper and guide for the journey. We do it in her bedroom, clean and cozy. I'm a little disappointed that there are no magical artifacts or dangerous-looking items of magic hanging on the walls. I smile to myself and think:

Really? Is that what I was expecting to find here?

This is my fairytale personality coming out. I was hoping my guide for the journey was going to be a powerful witch with ominous artifacts hanging from the ceiling and glowing eyes of animals lurking in the shadows.

Doubt is creeping in. Can she hold space for me? I look into her eyes, shining with light and caring. She is a beautiful elder – warm, kind, calm. She asks for my reason for coming here. I tell her I've never done ayahuasca before, that I feel like I've done everything else I can so far on my journey – I explored and embraced my shadow, I let go of all the abuse that had been done to me, I dedicated the last twenty years to doing all kinds of talking therapies, bodywork, yoga, NLP, hypnosis, meditation, breath work, regression, trance dance… but despite all the effort, time, tears, forgiveness, I am still restless, still looking. I tell her I feel like I've hit a dead-end and don't know what else to do. I'm in the darkness of the unknown. It's uncomfortable and it doesn't seem to want to go away. I don't know what to do next. If I only knew, I would do it. I'm not sure what ayahuasca has to offer but I'm open to receiving. She smiles and says:

"I see you have the right attitude, you'll be fine."

I hear a kind of knowing in her voice that's beyond time and space. I smile back. I want to trust her. I take one last look at her white hair and shiny focused eyes of an elder. Maybe I can.

Later that evening, we all gather in a large yurt. The fire makes soft crackling noises, it's nice and warm, and everybody in the circle is wearing white. Anarim is silent, smiling lightly. I'm sweating under my armpits – a clear sign that I've been stressing for a while now. People look like they're a bit apprehensive, but also eagerly awaiting the journey beyond the known, into their shadow, into their light. Everything seems to want to come to a stop. Suddenly, Anarim breaks the silence with his slow, deep voice:

"You probably have a lot of questions. The only thing you need to know is to surrender. We are very good at navigating this spaceship. Just keep letting go."

That's it, no other instructions, no list of rules, no fire exits.

That night I died.

Everything I knew changed forever (again).

Trust and surrender became my new mantra.

Carried violently by the mother medicine, in the middle of the night, completely unexpectedly, in my visions, I meet Kirt. How strange. But it's him. I know it, just as I know my name is Aya. We are two fluorescent centipedes dancing and twirling around each other in some dark spaciousness. I know, not much of a vision, Ididn't get the meaning of it but decided not to judge. I'm cultivating an approach to accept what is given. Try not to question, just let it be. So – two fluorescent centipedes twirling in a dance.

The next evening, people mingle in small groups, connecting, talking, sharing stories of healing, terror, and hope, warming up the November coldness with herbal teas. I walk into the kitchen and there he is, sitting with his back to the entrance, almost naked, wearing something that used to be a tee but is now made out of more holes than fabric. Is he wearing shorts? Can't see. Something about his shoulder makes my heart smile. I bend over and kiss it – an impulse that completely bypasses my rational mind. I surprise myself actually and get a bit shy. But there he is, receiving the kiss in the most playful way. He says:

"Wow, I really loved that, can you do it again?"

His voice is innocent and joyful, my thoughts melt, and I kiss him again, giggling as he moans in delight.

All this happens totally publicly, but in that moment, it's like the whole world ceases to exist. There is nothing and no one but us. Such a deep tantric connection from the first touch, such a strong energy able to open the gates to infinity in a blink of an eye. Wow. That moment releases my reservations for this man; my dish was empty from fear and now it's slowly starting to fill with curiosity.

The community in the kitchen receives us with giggles. Phew. It can be so awkward to suddenly realize you aren't alone when you've done some crazy, stupid thing. I tell him about my centipedes-vision and for some reason, he becomes obsessively interested.

We were wildly attracted and curious about each other, but we both knew this wouldn't progress any further. He was in a relationship with his goddess and I was totally not interested in him. Definitely and absolutely. So just before leaving the yurt, we casually swapped numbers. Everybody was swapping numbers and collecting emails, and I went with the motions, not expecting to hear from anyone. I was wrong. Kirt sent me a message via WhatsApp two days later – a playful little thing. I responded with a voice memo, since what else could I do? I'm a diehard sound healer. Sounding is what I do. Why would I use written words when I can use the sound of my voice – the different melodies, tempos, rhythm, breath… all of that to convey my mood, attitude, thoughts, and feelings?

He loved my message. He got so excited he recorded one back, and he enjoyed it too! From then on, we exchanged voice messages daily. Not a single day went by without at least a few hellos, updates, questions, cheeky jokes, crazy stories. We became best mates. Voice messages allowed us to explore a deeply intimate relationship without ever making love. Oh my God, wasn't that the most amazing relationship ever!

The Calling

It was a casual, unmemorable moment. I was sitting in my living room, legs up, nothing happening. And then I heard the calling. How does one hear the calling? Not with the ears, that's for sure. I was scrolling through Facebook and suddenly stopped at one particular event post. Something deep inside of me gave a big sigh and something else smiled. I just knew I had to be there. That's what I think people mean when they say in their ads, "if you hear the calling." I've actually used this phrase myself a few times in my event descriptions. It sort of indicates that only sensitive people, spiritual people, people capable of hearing the calling can come to the gathering. I know, I sound a little sarcastic. But making a gathering special is an important ingredient of any ceremony. That's what I thought then anyway, although my feelings about this have changed since. My feelings about ceremonies have also changed. Along with my understanding of sarcasm, funnily enough.

Sarcasm is a very interesting thing. It can be so funny, it can be so negative. It's such a diverse thing, sarcasm. I see it used to protect the heart. People are afraid to be vulnerable, to expose the soft, gooey, tender fragileness within, and use sarcasm as a shield to avoid pain and suffering. I think the heart knows no suffering. The heart is ready to take it all, everything and anything, just like our planet. The heart is capable of forgiving the unforgivable. The mind, on the other hand, is slow. The mind demands justice. It's there to defend the ego by any means necessary. It's a fully-armored ministry of defense in our United States of My Unique Identity. Don't get me wrong, the mind is important in our social lives, in keeping us safe and many other ways. But when it comes to living, full power, who you really are, the mind is a bit of an obstacle. You actually need to include your heart, and other parts if you want that. I come to equally value my mind and heart, and pussy for that matter. This is the holy trinity for me: mind, heart, vulva.

So anyway, I heard the calling to join a retreat with my Native American teacher, Naren. It was a pilgrimage with fellow seekers. Actually, I'm not entirely sure what everyone was looking for – some seemed more confused than others – and to be honest, I was confused myself. Anyway, it was a pilgrimage, a journey within, and the goal was to build a sacred labyrinth.

Naren was creatively using his sharpies and flip chart as he explained the old wisdom of the medicine wheel, spirituality, and magic of the labyrinth. He's a gifted teacher. He can weave facts, legends, and personal life stories together in such a beautiful way, and people are enchanted to open fully to the wisdom he conveys.

I really love my teacher, who I've been following for almost two years now. We once spent a whole day on Arthur's Seat in Edinburgh, sharing stories of passion, love, and freedom. Every time he spoke, I completely lost my sense of time and space and was fully submerged in the world he was creating. I always need a moment to come back and recompose myself. When I tell him my stories, he listens with such attention that it feels like there's a gravitational pull for my words, which form tiny tornadoes landing gently in the space of his perception. You know when you spend time with someone and it's just so great, and suddenly it's getting dark and you don't know how it got so late all of a sudden? That's my relationship with my teacher. Full devotion and time travel.

Today I was learning that a labyrinth can be male or female. The male labyrinth is one with many dead ends, forcing you to be focused, purifying your intention and strengthening your will. You achieve this by going back and forth many times. The female labyrinth is different. It has one way in, going round and round, all the way to the center. When you walk it slowly and mindfully, in meditation, in a ceremony, it can be a truly profound experience. The rule is that before you enter the female labyrinth, you must first go through the male one. You get lost before you find your center.

It's the first morning of the retreat and I'm so excited. All this is so up my alley. I love self-reflection, being outdoors, learning by doing. And we're all building something sacred! Conversations are minimal, everybody is turning inward. There's an option to go even deeper with this work, to fast with water only, and I'm all in! Three days of physical work on just water. Hmm… but then again, my body won't use energy for digestion, my senses will sharpen, everything will become clearer and more intense.

I want this. I'm ready for a serious breakthrough.

And of course, the universe responded.

One really has to be careful what one wishes for. It always comes, and always in unexpected ways! And there are always some painful lessons along the way.

For as long as I can remember, what I wanted most in the world was freedom and unconditional love. I was ready to pay any price for it, even to die for it. And I was mercilessly put to the test with my intentions time and time again. Going from a muddy path to a river full of crocodiles, to a tsunami, to a desert island…

I'm hungry and tired, walking in the woods and looking for rocks I can pick up and carry back to the meeting point. That's been it, all day. Sweat, confusion, doubt. Back to the woods. Back to the meeting point with more rocks. I definitely don't have clarity and I'm not sharp. Just really hungry and desperately miserable.

Wow, I'm so stupid, I'm paying a lot of money to walk in the woods, experience pain, and be hungry. Well done, Aya, great fun! You could have gone on a proper holiday, enjoyed yourself, gotten a tan. But I wanted this. I'm here. Just trust and surrender. Accept and embrace. Accept what – that I came here to suffer? What's the point? It's just hard. Life is hard. Even when it's comfortable.

A few tears roll down my cheek. I start singing a song. Just a simple song I learned somewhere before.

"Earth my body, Water my blood, Air my breath and Fire my spirit."

I keep singing on a loop. I sing even when I see someone else close by. I notice that people around me are also exhausted and struggling. And I keep singing. To their red faces and shiny drops of sweat.

"Earth my body…"

As the day advances on us, I slowly disintegrate.

"Water my blood…"

Aya, the girl walking in the woods, the young warrioress on a spiritual quest with her teacher, slowly cease to exist. Aya the hunger, Aya the pain in her back and hips, and even Aya the song slowly disappears. All that's left is intent. To carry on with the currents of this space and time, to be in the moment.

And I make it to the end of the day. Phew. Some people are sharing fresh organic food in the kitchen. I'm not eating, but I'm so hungry. I think there will be a ceremony after sunset and I'm looking forward to gathering around the fire with everyone. I'm disappointed to hear there will be no such fire, no sharing. A gust of anger reaches my stomach.

Shit. But I need it.

I'm realizing just how hooked I am to ceremonies. I love them, I look forward to them, they bring me comfort, they make me high. I feel connected, I feel loved, I feel the presence of something greater than me. Hmm… okay. I park this idea for later. I can't deal with Aya-the-ceremony-junkie now. This moment is just so intensely saturated with everything, it's overwhelming. I feel I've reached every possible limit of what I can take, physically, mentally, and emotionally. Shower and early bed, then. Better to disappear in sleep than carry on with this struggle to awaken.

On the second day, I wake up with a splitting headache. I see the beautiful blue sky and am angry with it because it hurts my eyes. I hear a soft murmur of a stream nearby and hate its invitation to have an amazing day outdoors. I want to hide, or better yet, leave. I want everything to disappear. I walk slowly to the toilet, my legs heavy. The loo is beautifully designed with deep blue-green colors, heavy mirrors, a stone floor, inspiring spiritual books at hand. I sit on the toilet and want to cry. I'm so unhappy. Every fiber of my being is screaming:

No!

I hate this experience. I hate this moment.

Why am I here again?

I have no answer to that.

I go to the kitchen and make myself an herbal tea. My legs are stalling. I want to fool my stomach with this tea, but it's no idiot, it knows this isn't food. I'm trying hard to keep my tears inside. I swallow them. Lokantina joins me. She is also fasting. She looks as miserable as I feel. We don't talk, just sitting there silently. Somebody is making coffee and the beautiful smell of a dark roast is filling the space, waking everyone up. Slowly, people are gathering, and it looks like we're about to start another day of gathering rocks – sweat and pain. I don't even know what to think anymore. And suddenly it hits me. I'm working like a donkey, hungry and unhappy building something for these wealthy people! I tapped into my ancestral trauma! How about that? So much anger, so out of proportion.

I look at the facts: I love my hosts, a lovely couple, trying to strike a balance between having resources, sharing them, and discovering spirituality. Yes, they are wealthy, yes, they have a gardener and cleaner who come every day to keep the grounds tidy. Yes, they have beautiful artifacts they bought while traveling through every corner of the Earth. I'm happy for their prosperity, for this amazing big house and garden with a stream running through it. I'm happy for them to be able to afford to pay people to keep it nice for them. Honestly, it isn't about them personally. But I have this hatred, this deep resentment about being hungry and suffering in the process of building something for them. It's about my great grandparents and their parents, working and dying for wealthy land and factory owners.

My ancestors came to the rapidly growing city of Łódź before the second world war. A city that was being populated and built mainly by Germans, Jews, and Russians. They say that the Germans brought technology and know-how, the Jewish brought money, and the Russians brought culture. And they thrived there, building what's now the third biggest city in Poland. This area used to have twenty rivers flowing through it, making it an ideal setting for the textile industry. Chasing money and growth had a disastrous effect on the environment and humans alike. The manufactory workers earned just enough to keep their heads above water, but no more. My ancestors were in that crowd. Fancy clothes, restaurants and theatres, were not accessible for them. And in those days, if you had an accident and say, lost your arm, it simply meant you were no longer able to do your job. You were fired, that was that. No insurance money or anything. One day you just go bust, unable to feed your family.

All these stories come rushing through. More stories

of working on the land and dying young with fever, dying young while giving birth, losing family members to hard circumstances… my eyes fill with tears and my heart with loving compassion. I understand now. My ancestors went through a lot. But I'm not my ancestors. I don't have to live in this shadow. I can decide to end this suffering now. So I dedicate this day to them. With every rock I carry, I send them love and light. And when the day is over, I eat for them all. No more hunger for my ancestors. They can all rest now. And that's how the shadow of this timeline ended. Accepted, acknowledged, embraced, and put to rest.

This evening, we work until very late at night. We've finished the structure and it looks amazing, the rocks gently reflecting the moonlight. The labyrinth rests between two trees. and it feels like they're the natural guardians of this sacred space.

That night, I close my eyes in silent surrender and something in me dies. And then I am reborn.

On the third day of the retreat, we prepare for a celebration and ceremony. Firewood is gathered, the half-moon altar is decorated with flowers, bark, seeds, and prayers. New people arrive to join us. It's getting dark and my teacher isn't there. People sit around the unlit bonfire. Everyone's chatting, and it feels like a space outside a pub in east London rather than a sacred space minutes before a deep shamanic journey.

I close my eyes, grab my drum, and just breathe for

a moment. I start drumming and humming gently to the beat.

What the hell am I doing? I'm no shaman.

But the drum is inviting me to carry on. Bah-bah-dum bah-bah-dum. I'm not doing it because I'm a shaman, I'm doing it because it feels right. Yes, I'm feeling the calling again. My inner dialogue gives up. And I put all my attention to singing, now happening much louder with all sorts of vowels and a clear melody. For a while I just flow with it, allowing it to carry me, effortlessly. When I finish, everyone is silent. And the silence is listening. The teacher is back and the ceremony starts.

Many rounds of songs, offerings, and sharing later, I walk barefoot through the labyrinth. I slowly circle the path, fully embodying every movement. When I reach the center, somewhere deep within me, a door opens.

Yes, I am this human being, and this is my path…

Hoka Hey

I bow my head again, touching my forehead to the ground as I crawl inside the sweat lodge. Inipi, Temazcale – this ritual has many names and many traditions. It's the womb of the Great Mother. You go in to shed old skin, leave old ego, release old habits and limitations. You stand at the edge of the great void. And then you come back and you present yourself to the sun – fresh, cleansed, renewed. You feel reborn again, and you receive the blessings from the fire for the journey ahead.

I crawl on all fours, whispering:

"Hoka Hey! Let's do this."

The structure is tiny. Claustrophobic even. You can't stretch. You're down in the dirt the whole time. As you crawl in, you drop onto the floor, drop your armor, your spear, your shield. Your knees, feet, and hands are deep in the moist, cold, grassy surface of the planet. You can smell her. You can whisper to her. Give her your thanks, tell her your name. Slowly, you get to your spot. You sit tightly in a circle. It's very dark, with the only light coming from the tiny door you came through. Soon the door will close. The shaman is waiting for the last person to settle. Everybody is here to do something important. I look around. This is the last time I'm able to see the faces. Women are on the left, men are to my right. The door closes.

There are many different ways to conclude the ritual of a sweat lodge, but the essence is that you are here, sitting with your fears in total darkness as it grows hotter and hotter. Your ears are burning and you think you can't take any more. Your shoulders are burning too and it's very difficult to take a breath in. Drumming. Singing. You're in and out of trance. You can dig your fingers deep in the earth, which brings coolness. You can pray, which brings focus and calmness. Remember why you're here. Remember who you are. But the fear is so strong. How can you let go?

I hear men singing to my right and I think about all the men in my life. Whispering to the earth in my hands, I give them thanks. I think about nature; the birdsong and the swaying of the trees that remind me of her loving nature, and I give thanks to them. I think about all the women here and out there that became mothers and I send them deep gratitude. All women for whom motherhood was never a part of their life, and I send them my sisterly love. For the fathers and mothers – thanks to them, we are here. For healing wounds.

Tears come flooding. Pain envelopes me, physical and emotional.

I came to this world so innocent and so pure. All love. I knew nothing of the rules of this world. I had my soft gooey heart in my hands, offering it to people around me. My mum. My dad. But they smashed it painfully and violently. My tiny little red heart in my hands. Bleeding. So I hid it, deep inside, covering it in layers and layers of anger, cynicism, verbal violence, strong boundaries.

All those years later, thanks to the helping claws of heyoka, traveling, relationships with men and women, and sound – here I am with my heart out again, offering it to the people around me. My friends, my lovers, my family. But it's still a very scary thing to do. I put my head on the ground and surrender completely. Tears flow directly into her. I am grieving. For all that time I wasted on fear and anger. For all the people who would like to open, but can't. For not being met in that space.

How Are You, Aya?

Howard is a good client of mine. He appreciates my workshops, pays what we agree on, is always on time, and books more workshops in advance. A clean and tidy business partner. I like it. And I love him. He's such a beautiful, kind, and clean human being. There's no stickiness in our relationship, no expectations to be someone or do something else, no hidden deals. I look at his question via WhatsApp and feel a crowd of thoughts, words, stories in my mind, all ready to be vocalized, to be expressed and released. So without thinking much, I press record on my phone and start a voice message.

"Hey, Howard, I was just putting my boots on, my dog is looking at me attentively, because he is sensing we are going for a walk, but I reckon he can wait for me to record this message to you. I came back from India a few days ago and it's so wobbly. I've been there long enough and I changed so much, but the settings here in Bristol are asking me to be the Aya I was before I left and there is a tension within me, because I don't want her back. Well, I'm happy to be organized again, focused, but I really want to keep my heart fully open, and be spontaneous, chatty, and wild, like in Goa. So there's a bit of negotiation happening now to find new terms for being Aya."

"India was absolutely magical. Very inspiring, lots of things happened. I fell in love with a guru and tantra master and he robbed me of my identity and took all my money. I mean I gave him £3600 freely, and I followed him everywhere. The experience with him was very psychedelic without the use of any substances. Everything was so strange and so magical. I traveled beyond my limits so many times. And then that was it. I had £2 on me, my debit cards maxed out, my credit cards maxed out, and I was like… fuck. I told him he has to give me back my money, because you know, he borrowed it, said he was going to give it back once his American card gets unblocked, and I believed him. I was on a bowl of rice for three weeks prior to that, literally eating rice for dinner to save money. I wasn't spending money on anything else either… not going anywhere, not doing anything. I just meditated all day, every day, because that's free. I slept in the cheapest hostels I could find in Bangkok – £3 for a bunk bed in a ten-bed dorm, breakfast and coffee all day included. Never complained. Patiently waited for him to tell me he's got the money. And I was grateful. I treated this as a gift, an opportunity to spend more time with myself, no distractions; an opportunity to go very deep with my meditation practice, to be humble and grateful for the abundance I experience in my life. But when I had £2 left, I had no choice but to be assertive. And prior to that, I asked him for my money few times, always in a sweet, innocently inquiring voice. But this time it was time to talk dates and numbers. I needed a plan. I wasn't in agreement with what would happen next without money – to sleep rough on the streets or to beg for food. And he said:

"You are so unenlightened with your money. You have a really bad relationship with it, you hold on to it.'"

"And I was like, wow, I gave you everything I had, I have nothing. And that's when I finally realized, he is fake. If he was who he claimed he was, he would be able to see me. I also realized that our journey together was over. I didn't say much though. I just asked him again to give me back my money, that we had an agreement and I wanted him to conclude. But instead, he said he doesn't want to speak to me or see me anymore. He said I'm bad energy. It was so hard. Full-blown shit storm. Actually, it felt like somebody put me in the bullet blender with a lot of smelly cat shit and pressed the button. I could no longer tell what was what. And you know what? I know now that I invited myself to it. Nobody made me. I walked in that smelly layer of death and destruction with my own free will."

"With my £2, I went to my favorite vegan cafe close to Khaosan Road. I was tearful and shaky. A woman sat at my table, she was in Bangkok for the jewelry fair. I tried to have a casual conversation with her, but I ended up telling her my story. And a miracle happened. She said she double-booked her hotels when she was planning her trip. She tried to cancel one of them, but they kept coming up with rules why she couldn't, so she gave up. She offered the spare room to me, just asked me not to use the minibar and not to make damages, as they have her credit card details and will charge her for everything... wasn't that just what I needed! I took it, I spent four days and four nights in a beautiful air-conditioned room on the top floor with an amazing view of the city and the sunset. A lot has happened for me in that room, the most important thing of all, I realized I have a story to tell. A story of pilgrimage, spiritual awakenings, romance, and heartbreak! Stories that took me to unconditional love and freedom. And the stories are exciting, because they include this crazy guru and a porn star, the Native American Church, sisterhood, betrayal, and romance... I invested straightaway: 0.30p for a pencil and notebook – and I was set and good to go!"

I finish my voice message to Howard, thanking him for asking me how I was, grateful to have an opportunity to voice my story. He responds to my message in a kind and beautiful way, offering support and mentoring, saying he's also written a couple of novels and actually helps writers professionally. Another synchronicity. That's how it is now. People appear in my life when I need help. And it's not about money – never has been.

The Masculine Push & Pull

Every time I meet a man who could be The One – my lover, companion, guardian, warrior, friend, and partner – I make a deal with myself. I hide away the parts of me I think he might dislike. It happens instantly, the moment I connect this particular man to my dream of being together forever. It happens in a very subtle way, on the edges of my awareness. Something in me makes a judgment that he will absolutely despise my messiness and chaos, that he will be petrified of my wild side and won't like my intimate connection with nature and spirituality. In the snap of a finger, it's all gone, hidden deeply under a fluffy carpet of a smile. It happens unconsciously, always does. It's only recently that I've developed an awareness of just what I'm doing to myself. I mean, I'm turning forty this year. It's taken me a while, picking up the pieces. A recent relationship breakdown put the last puzzle piece in its place and finally, I understood.

I was the cruel one – I wanted it finished and he didn't see it coming. It was a complete surprise and shock for him to hear me say:

"I love you, but I cannot be intimate with you anymore."

That was exactly how I felt. It was so weird – one day, everything as usual, walking the dog in the park together, giggling, enjoying a meal, talking about work, snuggling on the sofa. The next day, I have no desire to open to that man anymore. Like the end of a show. Curtain down, lights off, nothing more to see here, go home. It was so surprising to me that I wanted to take time to check in with myself.

Is this state temporary? What's going on here?

So I gave myself time to be with this, rest in it, explore all the sensations, let them be. No judgment. This is just what my mantra says:

Let go and surrender.

The more I allowed myself to feel those feelings, the more I grew in confidence that I didn't want to be with this man. Everything about him stopped being attractive to me. How bizarre. I was deeply confused. My rational mind was telling me:

I love this man, we've been together for the last year, living together, exploring shamanic practices together, pray-

ing, connecting, looking after each other, inspiring each other to grow, dancing, making love... what the hell?

But if there's one thing I trust fully and completely in my life, it's my guts and my pussy. Yes. And my pussy was closed for business. No tingling, no pulsing, no moistening. Door closed and locked, lights off, nobody home. Of course, he noticed straight away, being so close. He wanted to know what was happening. How could I tell him? I didn't even understand what was going on with myself. He was such a caring, gentle man, he gave me the space I requested, just to receive my dreadful sentence at the end of my three-week silence.

"I love you, but I cannot be intimate with you anymore."

He was shocked, but not lost for words. He yelled at me full power, his raging spit landing on my face. I took it all in. Again, surrendering to the moment, I saw him as he was – hurt. For all he knew, he was doing the right thing; gave me space to process whatever I needed to process, patiently waiting for me to come back to him. He wanted to help me, to work things out together, to support me, but I requested time off and he respected that, hoping to connect again at the end of it. And now he was being rejected. As I witnessed this man's full-on adult tantrum, I was shaking. I honestly wasn't sure if he was going to hurt me – he was so violent with his words, his face red with fury. But in my core, I was very still and very calm. A quiet little voice reassured me I was doing the right thing.

It took us six months to actually part properly. I was committed to supporting him through the process, because I felt guilty and he was convinced that whatever I was going through would eventually pass – I'd come around, change my mind, go back to 'normal'. It was so hard. I totally get it when I meet people who refuse to be in relationships to avoid the heartbreak at the end. It's messy, it's painful, and it goes on forever… either you get your heart broken or you're the bitch that breaks theirs. Either way, it sucks. I was so sad to see his suffering. I painfully felt the dry seabed of tears he wouldn't let out. I was annoyed and frustrated and taken beyond my limits with the constant:

"Why?"

Again and again…

"I don't know why, I just know what – I don't want to be with you anymore."

He made me break up with him so many times, it was like self-inflicted torture. Why don't I leave now? Come on, that's enough, leave this man, disappear. But the same source that closed the door on him wanted me to support him through this transition. I had to stay. I loved this man. I caused his suffering.

"What can I do?"

And he would look at me, deepest longing in his eyes, and say:

"Tell me why."

Arghhh… that one I don't know!

So much anger and guilt. The whole situation felt so sticky. I just wanted to get out. But I had to stay. Let go and surrender. Yes, my mantra. It's making me insane.

Why am I doing this to myself?

I looked him in the eyes and explained again that it was nothing he'd done.

"It's like switching off the lights, there's just nothing there anymore."

He couldn't believe it.

"How can it be? Something must have caused it."

He's so stubborn. Just as stubborn as I am. Checkmate. No further moves.

I believe that every relationship, romantic or not, happens for a reason. And actually, a few years later, I came to the conclusion that the purpose of this particular relationship had come to fruition. I supported this man to release and let go of his ex-wife, kickstart his healing process with his father and the family. In return, he inspired me to get formal training in sound healing, as he saw my gifts clearly when I didn't. He was the reason I got my certificates.

That was done. And we were done. Six months of drama and I was free again. He moved out and made an effort to move on. And suddenly, I was flooded with new knowing; it hit me how I chose to be a soft, warm, fluffy woman for him. I had locked away my violent winds because I thought he'd hate them. It was perfect. He needed a nurturing and healing relationship and I needed the experience of locking myself in for a man. Again. But it wasn't sustainable. I would never be able to keep my wild nature locked away forever. It would come out, sprout up in moments and situations, grow like vines around our everyday moods and conversations.

It's almost midnight. I'm standing on top of a hill, cheeks wet from my salty tears, reuniting with the totality of myself. Realizing one more thing: the reason I am not fully standing in my power is because I'm afraid of the far ends of my dark side. The person from my childhood who had the ultimate power – physically, emotionally, everything! – was my father, and he was not a good man. He was abusive, manipulative, and cruel. And I was afraid I'd turn out to be just like him.

I am like him.

To think I'm not like him at all is a denial. But I'm so much more than that. I'm able to rest in my feelings – they don't control me. I can take time and choose my actions. And more often than not, I respond to situations with love and compassion – not anger, fear, hatred. I am capable of being selfless – didn't I just prove it in the last six months?

I feel an energy release. This is another awakening

moment. On top of the hill, under a starlit sky, the tears now reaching my collarbones, I am waking up to claim my full power, all of it, light and dark. No more hiding away, no more sacrificing any part of my being for a romantic relationship. Let them see the totality of me. Give them a chance to love the whole of me. And me too – I also want to see the far edges of my darkness. I want to have the courage and opportunity to look. And, as usual, when you make such bold prayers, especially when you have trees, wind, river, and moon as your witness, the universe provides…

I refused to consider Kirt as a potential partner or lover from the moment I saw him, and we became close friends. For eight months, we spoke every day, so he got to witness all parts of me – no hiding away, no faking the girl I thought he would want for life. And I got to witness many of his sides too.

We were in the second week of our exciting interactions when I developed a curiosity about what he did for money. He seemed to have a lot of time on his hands, at different times of the day. He knew an awful lot about all the spiritual gurus and personal development authorities. He knew a lot about everything we'd spoken about so far: travel, sex, tantra, religion, economy, history, philosophy, business, marketing, cars, UFO… everything. He asked me what I was doing, and I told him about sound healing, yoga nidra, and the peer-mentoring charity I was managing at the time. He was blown away just how busy

I was and laughed at me for racing with the time. At first, I didn't want to know what he did – everything about this man was so extraordinary, I was afraid to discover that he had a normal job. I sat with my inquiry until my curiosity won out. I pressed record on my WhatsApp.

"Hey, Kirt, what are you doing for a living? Hang on, don't tell me. I want to guess. You are definitely self-employed, because you have free time during various times of the day and week, and you don't seem like the kind of guy who could withstand the routine in life that comes with working nine to five… I also think that you are doing something unusual and quirky, cheeky even."

I was thinking out loud. And then I said:

"Are you a porn star?"

It came in the spur of the moment, so I was surprised to have said that, but so far in this friendship, we were exploring boundaries in our communication, and to both our surprise and delight, there were no limits to what we could say. Nothing was off the table. The real cheeky moments were super fun and became gems in our conversations. I must say, everybody who has the ability to be in such freedom with me instantly becomes my family member, I value it so much.

So I threw in my wild porn guess, more of a joke than anything else, and was curious how he would react. I was already giggling when I got a message back. He said:

"Yes! You are not far from the truth."

How about that? I was shocked and so excited! Never before had I had a friend who was a porn star! Ha! Straightaway, my thoughts traveled to inquiring whether or not he would ever try to recruit me, and I couldn't decide what I would do if he did! I mean, I would be devastated if he didn't –

Am I not pretty enough? Not sexy enough? My tits too small? Maybe my nose too big? How about my pussy? Is she nice-looking?

Yeah… all those questions…

I would probably, most definitely, say no anyway. But I would love to be asked. Does that make me narcissistic? And vain? I definitely don't want to be either of those.

So I dismissed all the thoughts. Put them to rest. Killed them for good. Decided I would never come back to the matter again. Unless he tried to recruit me – then I would have a big problem to face. Because I just loved the idea of that kind of adventure – to be able to completely let go and lose myself in the passion of love-making with a man in front of the camera, in front of a whole lot of people watching, holding microphones, being aroused… yeah, the goddess in me was definitely interested in having an audience of people who were turned on, experiencing temporary difficulty with swallowing, wanting to touch me, smell me, completely lose control with me. Hmm… that was interesting, I hadn't known that about myself before Kirt. I mean, twenty years ago, in my home city, sharing this fantasy with friends would've made me a slut. I would have that label for life and probably have to spend the rest of my time in isolation or with other sluts, in some kind of Christian prison. But things had changed, no? I could keep my fantasy and freedom at the same time. Not that the fantasy was likely to materialize… but who knew?

So as you can see, Kirt's personality and his stories invited me to review a lot of my old assumptions, and not just about my sexuality. His fun, quirky, brilliant personality also invaded my spirituality, my life view, my work, and my relationships. My whole life!

Writing a novel is a funny thing. It sort of has a life on its own. I am witnessing the unfolding of this tale, one story leading to another, staying true to one constant thing in this process: my intention to touch you intimately by sharing the special moments of deeper settling in love, embracing the totality of life and merging with the divine feminine.

To my surprise, I come to realize that men are very much a central point in all of them. To be honest with you, I'm actually having a bit of a reaction to it. I love the strong women out there. I'm aiming to be strong myself: independent, beautiful, and self-reliant. I don't want men to be so important to me. Aren't we living in the *Time of the*

Sixth Sun[2] where women are supposed to lead the way? For a moment I think of re-writing my stories, focusing on something different. But the truth is that men have been and still are a powerful drive for change in my life, and for this, I am deeply grateful. I received so much from them, it feels really nice to appreciate them here. So I'm going to entertain you with a few more stories showing just how influential men can be.

The first man I slept with showed me I was a woman. It's true. Before Radek, I was very boyish – daring, erect, ready for action. Pushing forward whatever was going on within me at any given moment. Piercing through every situation, saturating it with my humor, ideas, and stories. I was a loud companion who people found either amusing or frustrating. Mostly people found me annoying, actually.

Radek was the brave prince who forged a way through the briar hedge, cut through thorns and bullshit, and woke me up to the fact that I was beautiful, complex, wild, and fierce. When I lost my virginity with him, I was no longer the sleeping beauty. I was an Amazon woman, riding on his cock freely, even if just for a short moment.

I was only able to do so because of his caring attitude, his guidance, acceptance, and loving encouragement. I let him in and he kindled the idea of a man and a woman

---

2 Time of the Sixth Sun is a docu-drama about the awakening and transformation of global consciousness. Available online.

coming together; how empowering it could be for both. It was December 1996, and those seeds were planted deep in my belly. Unconsciously, they stayed there until spring 2010, when they finally found the perfect climate for germination. I sure took my time, huh?

My second lover pushed me to break the chains of my family drama. I grew up in a home ruled by the need to drink. Everything spiraled around alcohol, there was nothing more sacred than that. The entire home was a living altar for this god we all worshipped. Depending on the flow of the sacred nectar, I tiptoed and tried my hardest to be invisible to avoid beatings, or else to avoid fuzzy and smelly outbreaks of fake love and appreciation.

The god of alcohol is a bit nasty, I can tell you that. Everybody in my family worshipped that deity in their own unique way. But despite our efforts, it always ended the same; with arguments, loneliness, and the ultimate poverty.

The truth is, we were all at the mercy of ever-changing moods, violence, and emotional manipulation. I was deeply ingrained in my role of a victim where my needs were constantly not met, where I couldn't allow myself to have any feelings, because if I let any of them in, the amount of anger, sadness, fear, neglect, shame, guilt, and confusion would crush and kill me. Only deep within did I nurture a tiny light of hope.

One day, all of this nightmare will stop. One day, my

mum will love me, we will spend time together, she will take time to listen to me and truly understand me. Maybe one day, we will be happy.

Every now and then, my hope would bring me to a crisis. I would realize this would never happen and I would be heartbroken, a complete mess without any energy to continue. Dull, numb, or crying. Like a zombie. What was the point of being alive? And then my hope would rekindle again. Hope. I just looked up the meaning of this word – Google says it's *an optimistic attitude of mind based on an expectation or desire; hope says in the future it could happen*. So hope is a prayer. It's something we have a deep desire to manifest, to live. It was my hope and my prayer for all those beautiful moments with my mum. And I was so blind. It wasn't true that my mother never loved me, never spent time with me, and never understood me. I just never had her the way I wanted – all for myself and sober. I shared her with her worries, desires, longings, pain, and fear. Alcohol was her medicine. I was a naive fool. My prayer was manifested all that time. And I was praying for the wrong thing.

I should have prayed to have her all to myself twice a week, haha.

Finally, one day, all of that mess came to a full stop. No, it wasn't when she died, bless her spirit. It was when I let go of fighting her alcohol, when I arrived at loving her as she was, with everything that came with her, including her addictions. That's when I found peace. True peace, freedom, and love can only come from within – there's no other way. But it took me a long time to realize this. Back in the times of big drama, every crisis was like an earthquake, threatening my whole existence. And every time it happened, I would complain to Joachim. I would indulge in telling him story after story of how cruel and mean this world was. We had this ritual of going for a walk with our dogs – a never-ending journey in the darkness of the late evening. His dog, my dog, sniffing wee on the grass together. Me complaining about my life, almost every evening for over a year. One time he simply told me:

"You need to get a job."

I couldn't see it happening. I was studying, hoping that the MA would change my life for the better. I was holding on to my course as if it was my lifeline. I saw it clearly in my imagination: I would make a big breakthrough with my research, true social change that could (and would) be applied in many systems for the benefit of all. My professor would beg me to stay at university, write more papers, spread the word, do TED talks. Students would love me for my passion, as money oozed from many different directions – publications, lecturing, social change projects… the sun would shine on me every morning when I'd drink my coffee, because it too would know just how good a life I was living.

Yeah, well, I had four more years before my master's thesis and final exams. A classic example of daydreaming when reality is too hard to cope with. Do you ever escape in perfect visions of the future when your present is unbearably shitty? The present moment for me then was sticky with doom and gloom. It was sad, painful, and argumentative. Joachim was right. He was yet another prince with a shiny sword that cut through my bullshit. He was cold and cruel, but he had to be, otherwise I wouldn't get the message.

"Face it. You hate uni and you don't have money. You need to move out of your home. You need a job."

And that's how it was. I knew he was right. Soon after this conversation, his mother moved to Israel for work and I was able to move in. I got a kitchen job in a small pub owned by two artists. This was a big shift in my life; I was in good company – drinking, yes, but at least these people weren't my relatives and didn't fight all the time. I was able to buy new shoes, which always helps. I made an effort to look nice going to work. It was good all around. It gave me a whole new perspective on family drama. I spotted a leaflet inviting grown-up children of alcoholics to therapy, funded by the state. Turns out it's nationally recognized in Poland that if you grow up with alcoholic parents, you'll be fucked up for life and need help. I know, alcohol is just one way to screw up your children, there are doubtless a thousand more. There are no programs for grown-up children of workaholics, broken marriages, infidelity, sudden deaths, moving towns, sudden change in family economy, severe mental health illnesses… I'm not complaining. I'm deeply grateful that the state recognized the need for therapeutic intervention to address trauma in adolescents and young adults. I'm sure they were hoping to build a strong driving force for a prosperous country, get to the head of the race. Who knew that a few years later, Poland would join the EU and all those young adults would choose to move rapidly to other countries like the UK, Germany, anywhere really. Most of our parents had been refused passports – they weren't able to travel or even visit family who perhaps emigrated during the war. You open the borders to the next generation and that's what happens, it explodes. And the investment of free higher education for the brightest ones, all the amazing projects of education in the wilderness to respect the environment, all that healing of trauma, goes abroad with us. But it's good. We live in a global village now – borders are only on maps. This is the gift of Poland if you dare to receive it, world.

So I committed to a nine-month program. I dropped out after six, but it was enough to kickstart a new life – one of seeking truth, finding *me*, connecting to the source. Gosh, it made me so lonely for so long. Who or what was me? That was a difficult question. I can tell you what it's not. Me or you, we are not the abuse we received, our economic status, what our partners see in us, our moods – shy, angry, scared, sad – our thoughts, the clothes we wear, what we let our friends see… none of that.

Right?

Over fifteen years of reading books, attending seminars, shamanic retreats, talking therapies, yoga, meditation, ecstatic dance, regression therapy, you name it, I was there… I only earned money to spend it on the project 'self-improvement'. I still didn't know who or what was *me*. But I became so good at healing trauma and looking my demons deep in their glowing, angry eyes. I was actively looking for more wounds to heal, and it became my obsession, my addiction. When I found an old wound, I would open it, clean it thoroughly, allowing pain and blood to flow freely, and then close it again, properly this time, with marigold and plantain for blessing and deep healing. The pain became my one true companion, my lover, the only constant thing in my life. One thing I could count on being there for me.

Quite morbid. Why did I not commit suicide? Well, I'm going to tell you a little healing secret here. There's a certain high that occurs when healing mental and emotional wounds. Every time I close a wound, I cut a tie. I sever an invisible thread connecting me with my perpetrators and traumatic circumstances. It's like cutting the ropes that anchor a hot air balloon on the ground. Every cut makes me feel lighter and freer. Every time I gain more insight about myself, I become more flexible with my life choices. When you cut enough ties, you come to a weird place indeed. The hot air balloon is no longer held by anchoring ropes. It will go in any direction, wherever the wind blows. You're free to do anything, react in any way imaginable to any circumstances. Just imagine you could stay indifferent to losing a job, being dumped, receiving a bunch of flowers from a good-looking stranger (honestly, can good-looking strangers do that more often, please? I mean, really, if you're good-looking, why not buy flowers and give them to people all the time? you never know what kind of effect it will have and how far it will go), missing your flight, seeing someone suffering. You're calm in all those situations, able to see all the different perspectives and choose wisely what you will do. Piotrek argues that this is just another word for being boring and having no personality whatsoever. I disagree. I think he says so because it's just too much work for him – he likes comfort and only makes an effort in his life if it brings immediate results. Like money.

"How much money is it going to get you?"

"None. But not everything is about money, you know."

"For you, nothing is about money."

He had a point. I couldn't argue with that. Besides, who said I was right with any of my opinions or ideas? They were just one person's perspective.

If you don't know where you want to go with your life, you can easily get overwhelmed. So I chose the direction of love and community, because that seemed to have a heart. It was a destination open to a wide horizon of possibilities. I wanted unicorns trotting up and down a rainbow, sprinkling gold stardust on the trees below. I wanted songs around the fire, hugs, organic food, giggles, creativity, colorful fairies, and passion. I wanted adventure and dragons, clear water and harmony.

But at the time, I was still addicted to pain and that kept me from achieving anything. The constant chase to find and heal the next wound was keeping me away from freedom. But I didn't know. I thought I was doing well; working on myself, growing, developing my consciousness. And I was succeeding. At least I had a purpose.

But this noble attitude made me narrow-minded and it became my trap. Rather than focusing on living my life, I was focusing on digging out traumas to heal. You get me? Everything in my life was serving the purpose of healing. That was the central point of the spiral I was in. Just another addiction. I made a list of all my bullies, all the people who had hurt me in any way. I examined each circumstance, one by one, reclaimed the power I had lost in each situation, forgave my perpetrators, and let go of the stories altogether. When that list was over, I created a list of every human being I came across and embraced all my experiences with them too. I was relentless, ready to go on like this forever. That's when I decided it was time to stop. Healing is a never-ending story. It's good to have a healthy balance there too. So I'm having an ongoing discussion with myself now, allowing everything to be as it is. After all, if I learned one valuable thing from all those ceremonies and shamanic experiences, it's to sit with the totality of my experience. Practice deep democracy with it. Not in dissociation and not in blind passion. Present. Engaged. When I feel like healing something, I do it with love and compassion, not out of necessity or obsession. But anyway, to go back to all the beautiful men in my life…

Kuchta saved me from HIV. At the time, I was still living with my parents, feeling acutely unwanted and unloved. I had such a deep longing for happiness and it felt so unavailable. Instead, there was a crack in the wall with a magnetizing darkness, lurking. Monsters were piling up in it; I couldn't see them, but I knew they were there. I had to fill it with something, plaster over it. One day, my girlfriend introduced me to a bunch of punks and hippies. They spent their days begging for change until they had enough to buy a couple of cheap wines. The local store was sensitive to their needs, kindly making sure cheap wine was always in stock. I wasn't even sure it was suitable for human consumption – I absolutely hated the wine and only pretended to drink it.

Just wet your mouth a little, don't take much in.

The trick was to vigorously tip the bottle to create some twirls of the red liquid inside.

I wasn't the only one who hated this drink. We're gathered around in a circle, drinking directly from the bottle, outdoors; everyone's complaining when it's their turn to drink again.

"Fuck, is it not finished yet?"

I really like being in a circle with them. I like their nice little ways. I love how close they are to each other, how they all support each other, complaining about the system and everything and everyone outside of their group; they have a strong bond and sense of belonging. They know they're in deep shit – all that poverty, homelessness, and lack of hope. I mean, seriously, they're the unwanted, dirty, and shameful margin of society in my city, but they're together. And they're a spiritual bunch too! Always giving the first little sip of wine to Mother Earth, with a little prayer. So I join them. They feel like a family to me. My first family outside of my birth family. Outside of our circle, we don't belong, we aren't valued or noticed. Within this family, we are together. And we're drunk. Soon enough, we swap alcohol with cannabis. It's hilarious. We spend hours and hours just laughing our bellies out. It gives me pain in my jaw, pain in my cheeks and my belly; seriously, this is really good stuff. I really enjoy it. It isn't so much about the content or the venue – I mean, we smoke in any sheltered public space we find suitable. It isn't so much about stories, problems, solutions. It's just about rolling on the floor laughing. So good.

But it doesn't last long. Cannabis is replaced with amphetamine. We sniff or take it with a drink at first (and then it's just *dance, dance, dance* for hours, or *talk, talk, talk*), but then we inject it directly into the bloodstream. Wow. I mean, wow. I just love these few seconds of rush.

This is the best thing ever.

My whole body is waking up, tingling, bursting with

energy and high. After the rush, I have nine hours of energy. I always tell myself I'll study for my A-levels, use that time constructively. All lies, I never do. And then a bad comedown, every time.

Doesn't matter. I like pain.

LSD is a nice change. Taken in between amphetamine, it always brings a night of wonder and adventure; exploring the woods, city, graveyards, whatever lies on our path.

What an amazing hidden world within my mind! Just change the chemistry in my brain a little and look what happens! Remarkable!

Shame you can't take LSD every night. I mean, you can, but it doesn't work so well. It's good to take a rest, give it a bit of time, and the next space-time travel is bound to be cosmic!

I come across a warning in the form of a man, a true star trooper, who took too many acids and lost it. He'll never stop tripping. Lost contact with what we call *consensus reality*[3] forever, no way back. You think it's funny? I think it is, sort of want that for myself, thinking *consensus reality is just so boring*. But he's a little scary. Can't keep the conversation going for too long, constantly getting distracted with invisible things (well, to be fair, they aren't in-

---

3 Consensus reality: the level of our experience that is measurable and shared – aspects of reality that we can reach a consensus about – Amy and Arny Mindell

visible to him), getting obsessed with random little ideas and thoughts that are traveling freely in the space-time around him – like satellites around a planet, his thoughts are able to become independent entities, valid and materializing around him, outside of his will.

Many years later I would be working with the homeless, addicts, mentally ill and criminal offenders. I am full of compassion and ideas on how to help. It's not just me – I'm surrounded by various support workers, recovery navigators, holistic therapists, and social activists. Everybody wants to help. And one day, I would pay a visit to the Bearpit Roundabout in central Bristol, a natural congregation space for rough sleepers. I want to talk, ask them what they need, what they want, what their solution to this problem is.

You know what I find? I'm reminded of my own history! It's so funny, I had completely forgotten about my own experience. I was thinking:

Different country, different times.

But human nature is the same, and so are the challenges of living in modern urban settings. If you're passionate about putting an end to poverty and homelessness, go spend a day with the representatives, listen to them, ask questions. You'll see them in a very different light. But more importantly, you'll see yourself in them like in a mirror. Scary, no? The people with multiple complex needs, as we call them, are a pain in the ass, because they show us the world is not a good place to live in. And that's painful to see, because we're responsible for it. Me, you, everyone.

When I was on the streets, I didn't care much about the outside world. The outside world was so wrong and so sick, I felt it was beyond hope. I thought we were the solution to the biggest problems of humanity: alienation and isolation. We were properly bonded, no shallow "Hi, how are you," and if you said you are feeling shit, they stared at you awkwardly, not knowing how to behave. Heart-brain-stomach bond. Communication going beyond sentences. We actually looked each other in the eyes and stayed open and responsive to body language. Honest and true, even if it meant risking being rude. We understood each other with no words (or so we thought, being in altered states of consciousness a lot of the time).

But it was pretty self-destructive. Just as my drug tribe started injecting heroin, I was incredibly lucky to meet Kuchta. He was my savior. Because even though I didn't like heroin with my first injection, I think one learns to like it after a few times. But Kuchta was against drugs. He despised drug users. And I fell in love with him. Completely and utterly. Okay, maybe I just swapped my addiction. Just maybe, I changed the way I wanted to fill the deep, dark gap. I no longer wanted to do it with drugs. I knew it wasn't good for me. Everybody knows, nobody's that stupid. It's just that we just can't see another way. Give us an alternative and we'll take it. But it has to be within what we can do at the time. You wouldn't expect a fish to play fetch, would you? Why would you expect a junkie to get a job? To be happy and compliant? To pay their bills on time? It's unrealistic.

Kuchta was such a blessing. He saw in me what I didn't. The sleeping beauty. My raw, unrefined nature, some kind of quality that sang a lullaby straight to his adventure-seeking nature. I think it was my thirst for freedom, but who knows. And he showed it to me in a sweet way – with his desire, his invitations, his caring for me. Ha! I was in a new loop with this amazing, beautiful man! I was so high on the falling in love thing with butterflies in my stomach, the withdrawal symptoms were minimal. Only the flashbacks were a bit problematic. Imagine us together having a peaceful walk in nature, when suddenly my body's going through a hit, just like when injecting. Hard to play it down. But possible. He absolutely despised drugs so I kept that part of me hidden from him. He lived a three and half-hour train journey south from Łódź. I was on that train every Friday evening, spending whole weekends with him, then back to school the other days. It worked. Only lasted a year, but come on, it was never going to be sustainable – after all, he was my addiction. But I got my A-levels. It was enough to enroll for a higher education degree.

One year later, I met my drug tribe a few times at funerals. Drugs were turning against people. Addiction is not a forgiving thing if you let it loose and ravaging. And people were receiving treatments for HIV. Fuck. I felt so incredibly lucky, blessed, and grateful. I mean, after two weeks of hell, when I was waiting for my test results... those two weeks of waiting for a possible death sentence were the end of my drug tribe for me. I never again let any substance take control of my life.

Goddess Rising

A lot of spiritual seekers know this one by heart. They heard it from a guru, yoga teacher, meditation master, and movies on Gaia TV. Everybody tries to get there, the non-dual reality, *Advaita.*[4] Nobody will admit it, not out loud – they know that to want to exist in Advaita is to have a desire, and that to have a desire is rooted in dual reality; you want it because you know you don't have it. You are experiencing both; a gap, a lack of something, and a necessity to change it, to have it. Desires are double-bad because they also mean you're not accepting your present moment! There's a lot of judgment stemming from that – if you don't accept your present moment then you're truly far from enlightenment. Your meditation practice is limping and your spirituality in general just sucks. That's if

4 Advaita Vedanta, literally: "not-two"; means non-dual and is a school of Hindu philosophy. This non-duality or oneness is a fundamental quality of everything. Everything is a part of and made of one non-dual consciousness.

you hang out with the Very Spiritual Guys who rub their bellies and talk only positive stuff in angelic voices. They say there is no two – the ultimate truth is non-dual, and we are all one.

I have a tricky relationship with Advaita. At times, I experience it to be real on such a profound level that I have goosebumps, the sensation of air coming down my lungs is pure love, and then my body disappears and sort of merges with everything that surrounds me – a kind of vibration, an all-filling presence. At other times, I am as far from it as one can be. Now is one of those times.

I'm sitting in a nice café. The tables are made of driftwood, beautiful, small hanging pot plants are dotted randomly, adding a nice green vibe to the air coming from the Arabic sea. It's not windy, just fresh. The sunlight is soft, coming from large window–openings in the wall. There are no windows here, just open spaces overlooking the beach. I feel tearful and sad, I don't know why.

Okay, just allow it to be.

But I'm indulging in my sadness, that can't be good!

There's judgment about your sadness and indulging. Just let that be also.

But then I'll be just sad and snotty, red and unattractive!

Let that be – the fear of being red and not sexy.

I'm doing my best to be with the totality of the present moment when a young couple enters the café. The girl is skinny and beautiful, her hair long and sleek, skin so smooth and nourished I want to put my cheek against it. She's sitting down in an armchair with her back straight. There's a lot of grace in how she moves, like a young queen. Her boyfriend has wide shoulders, his muscles showing through the thin fabric of his t-shirt. What a couple!

Is this even real?

I look around; yes, it's as real as anything else here.

They're not talking much, just looking outside. They are both so heavenly made, including their designer pastel summer clothes. Shoes, shades, suntan, the whole lot looking great – not too hipster, not lame, just super-fine.

My eyes wander outside to see what they're looking at and I see an elderly woman walking down the beach. She's wearing a swimsuit and a see-through sarong. Her belly is big and round, creating a large curve below the line of her breasts. Her body behaves like jelly, shaking a little as she puts her feet down going forward, her steps tiny.

This is so very interesting, this display of diversity of female form in front of my eyes, just as I was experiencing fear of not being attractive. Hmm… yes, now that I come to think of it, the subject of beauty has been present since this morning when I looked in the mirror and didn't like what I saw.

Is this me?

Those blemishes, little pink spots, freckles, imperfections – that's all I saw. Then I received a message from Kirt saying:

"We are not together anymore."

How many times is he going to break up with me? Honestly, this is ridiculous. Whatever, I don't care anymore.

Except that I don't. This is just something I told myself to cope with that moment. But the message was strong and painful. It landed in the bottom of my stomach. And it linked with the terrible morning face I saw in the mirror. It was an alliance that happened unconsciously, silently, in secret.

This is what happens to ugly girls – they get dumped.

But I wasn't aware of it. So I swallowed the break-up message, brushed my teeth, put some clothes on (whatever), and went to my morning meditation class. It was my daily practice at the time.

In the Shala, I meet many young beautiful women. Perfect skin, beautiful smile. I let out a big sigh, finding relief in the fact that I never considered myself pretty, so I don't have to compare myself with them. But I still do. Very quietly, in the dark corners of my mind, in a very cruel way, I take the best bits about them – a cute straight nose, naturally long and curly eyelashes, collarbones, neckline, whatever I deem extraordinarily beautiful – and compare them with my blemishes. And then all that's left to do, really, is dig a deep hole right where I stand and bury myself to release the world from my disgusting view. I'm an abomination to womankind, I should never pass on my ugly genes because I am a disgrace. As I think this, I laugh out loud.

Wow. Just a few blemishes and a tiny spot, and I'm ready to release the world from my view – what a powerful thought!

I really enjoy the little conversations I have with myself. This is certainly a side-effect of spending so much time on my own. But I like it. I mean, I listen to myself like nobody else. I give myself time like nobody else. When other people listen to me, they understand me through the lenses of their mood, their personal history, and previous experiences of similar subjects. Even when people really try to get you, they never can, not truly, because all they see is themselves in a mirror. Guess what? When I listen to myself, it's me, with my personal history and my relevant experiences. To understand yourself is probably the best thing you can do. So that's why I talk to myself. I'm still capable of knowing when not to, like in public places surrounded by people, or when I actually talk to real people. I'm not losing it, don't worry – try it for yourself.

So anyway, I'm sitting in this café by the beach, laughing out loud – it's Goa, people are either relaxed or high, they really don't mind, actually smile back at me. And then a shocking realization that my mood has changed dramatically. Just a moment ago, I was sad and tearful, ready to start digging a hole where I could die, ugly and lonely. Now I'm laughing. Yeah, that's the power of letting go, right here. Ever-flowing, ever-changing currents of feelings and thoughts. The trick is not to cling on to them, not to feed them and not to fight them. And they will come and go. Simple, no?

The next moment, I feel an invitation to indulge back in the self-pity, but the invitation is weak and soon fades away. I gaze at the far, simmering horizon of blue and blue and allow myself to get lost in it. The following morning, I wake up, have breakfast, and as the day goes by, I randomly receive lots of compliments – all about my beauty, how about that? At dinner time, I sit at La Plage, my favorite restaurant in North Goa, I'm on my own again, and I smile to myself with so much love and compassion, my eyes are wet.

24/04/2019

Today is my mum's birthday. I realized it just now. Not because I remembered – I never remember any meaningful dates, my phone told me. And suddenly, from being relaxed and easygoing, I become tense and absent-minded. That's the power of thought, right there. Nothing else happened, just remembering my mum, and wham! Sweaty hands and dark clouds in my mind, foreboding thunder and heavy rain.

It's her first birthday since she died.

But I dealt with her death so well, I think.

Why is it so hard now?

Here it comes again, the Why, my favorite, most useless mind game. But I'm aware of it, I catch it happening, so I have the power to change it. Okay, so I'm releasing the Why. I let it be. Dark clouds and sweaty hands it is then, tension and feeling spaced out. Let it all just be what it is.

For a moment, I just sit with it, and then all the stories rush through my mind and it feels like I'm in the ocean, going toward a storm in a boat the size of a walnut shell. The waves are crazy, going every direction and I hold tight to my walnut safety. This isn't really any kind of safety. The gravity of this story, the size of this storm, is overwhelming. I feel a need to expres this story out loud, to release it; I need someone to witness it. But I'm on my own again.

So I pick up my phone, open WhatsApp, and look at recent messages. Edgar. Oh my God, Edgar… yes, I met him only recently when I was in Goa, and we instantly had a deep connection. If Edgar was an animal, he'd be a black Friesian horse – majestic, beautiful, strong, with a wild temperament. I met him at the end of a group meditation practice. People came around and were talking. Edgar was saying how he just found out he has to minimize his eye contact with people in general because it makes them uncomfortable. A few people had complained to him just how uncomfortable his eyes were. A deep-sea diver made a somersault in my stomach.

Ha! I know exactly how it feels!

So I grabbed him and pulled him away from the crowd. Smiling from ear to ear, I asked him to gaze into my eyes. He was a bit surprised by the sudden request, but his curiosity won out and he gave it a go without a word. I watched him becoming completely engaged in just looking. His whole essence, all life energy focused in his eyes. Brown, big, shiny. So clear, so sharp, so strong, full of life energy.

Omg, what a delight!

I met him with my gaze. In an instant, it silenced my thoughts completely. My whole being electrified into nothingness. Energetic nothing. A void full of potential. Somewhere between my eyes and his, we tapped into infinity. And that was the end of dual reality around us.

This is how I met Edgar. I literally got lost in his eyes. We spent just over a month in Goa, sharing food, swimming, gazing, giggling. He told me about his meeting with a few thousand gurus who changed his life, showed me photos and videos he had made[5]. Wow, what an amazing story that was! He also told me about his twin flame experience that opened him to spirituality, about his family, his hopes and dreams, and in return, I besprinkled him with my stories. The rest was fertile, nurturing silence.

I love him so much. He is my tribe, my brother. Yes, he is the perfect person to release my emerging wave of feelings and memories. It's only appropriate. I'm not sure what the story is yet. So many memories crowd in the small bottle of my awareness, ready to pop. Should I try and focus on the positives? Or shall I narrate the drama? I'm such a drama queen. I don't really want to perpetuate those stories, feed them, make them stronger. Thoughts are so powerful, they really shape the life we live… okay,

---

5 Find Edgar's work on https://edgarbonnet.com/

stop. Should I this, should I that… this is nonsense. Take a breath, relax a little, let my thoughts be what they are…

Yes, spaciousness. With breath always comes spaciousness. The bottle is still ready to pop, but I give myself a chance for a little stillness around the edges. This is enough to reconnect with the trust I have in myself, in the core of me, in the unfolding of my journey. Trust and surrender is my mantra. So I allow this to happen, another breath, and I'm ready for the story to unfold in the way it wants.

"Edgar, my brother. I want to share something with you. Feel free to comment, or not to comment, whatever your feelings are, all is welcome. So… I just realized, like twenty minutes ago, that it's my mum's birthday. She died in May last year, just a few weeks after her last birthday. It was very sudden and unexpected. It's still quite fresh. But I'm okay with her death, honestly.

My mother used alcohol to self-medicate the pain that she felt. She was so sensitive and so vulnerable. I think she might have suffered depression. Looking at her, it felt like the hardship of life was weighing her down so much, making it unbearable to keep going. I was fighting her alcohol the best I could, all my life. I loved her so much and I saw the devastating effects of her medicine. I reached precision and craftsmanship in my negotiating, explaining, rationalizing, begging, avoiding, terrorizing… I used any method I could think of. She was not well and she couldn't see it. She would just smile that mom's smile that knows beyond her little daughter's capacity to understand the world. But with years, I saw her decline in cognitive skills, memory, her wellbeing, her ability to connect with people, including close family – every aspect of her life was affected, you know? Where was my beautiful, wise mom? It was such a big thing; I was willing to do anything. And it was going on for years and years and years… ever since I was a little girl, I was fighting her. In my twenties and thirties, my fight became so fierce I turned into a bad-ass terrorist. I asked her to choose: me or alcohol. Whenever I arranged to visit, I would call her in the morning and again on my way, and if I heard in her voice that she already drank that day, I would turn around and go back home. And she did. And I did. Almost every time. And I cried so much. I wanted my mum, you know? Not this confused, loud, talking nonsense wreck of a person. She must have missed me, I certainly missed her, why wouldn't she just not drink for one day? I was lost. I tried everything – to support her, to trick her, to force her… it was twenty years of my life, you know? Nothing worked. So then I focused on myself. I thought, hey, maybe I need to do the work somehow? So I started my journey of healing. To forgive her for not loving me, not being there for me when I needed. In the process, I discovered just how much I was blaming her for every failure in my life, wow. But I healed that too. And when I was done with her, I had to forgive myself for being such a shitty daughter, because I was. It was such a long process, you know? Years. But I did it. Most of it I was able to do myself. Whenever

I got stuck, I received help from shamans, healers, energy workers… regression therapy took me to past lives I shared with my mum, and I sorted out the karmic debt we had there too. And deep within me, there was this hope that one day, when I finished with my work, when I finally completed dealing with the backlog of mess in the space between us, somehow the energy would be released, air cleansed, butterfly effect, magic of the universe, whatever the mechanism, she would stop drinking. Right? All that time and effort. It has to have an effect! Well… no. It didn't. She never stopped.

I was devastated.

I was looking for more stuff to heal; surely, it just meant that I missed something, I just needed to look deeper! No. It was all done, there was nothing more to unpick in the relationship with my mother. But then something happened to me. This thought hit me that I just needed to completely surrender to the fact that I had done everything I could and that she and alcohol were together, always. I had to accept and welcome the whole thing. And it was so hard. Sitting with her and taking in her sadness, her alcohol-induced confusion, her drunk tears, her feeling of isolation even though she was sitting right next to me, knees touching. But it was also very sweet. Opening up to her, I saw her suffering, her guilt and shame, so much. I saw just how tired, fragile, and small she felt. And deep in her eyes, I saw that she loved me, and she cared for me. She just couldn't express it the way I wanted; it wasn't available for her. So heart-breaking and so beautiful. I cried for days. All that work I'd done was useful after all. The miracle did happen, just not the one I was aiming for.

The night before the hospital staff switched off her life support system, I was sleeping in my house in Bristol, on the sofa downstairs, cuddling my dog. Suddenly I was up, feeling fresh and rested, looking at my watch, it was 3:30 am. I felt my mum's presence. She was there with me in the living room. I could smell her, and I could sense her energy close by. And suddenly I was overwhelmed with intense, unconditional, unlimited, pure motherly love. Of course, she always loved me like that, she never didn't love me. Tears were flooding my cheeks, my whole skin was covered in goosebumps. Her life stories scarred her, conditioned her, limited her, and she never found a way through them. But on a cosmic level, all she ever felt for me was pure love. I spoke to her, to the darkness in the room: yeah, go mum, I totally get it, life has been so super painful for you and you want to go now, so go.

And that was it. We exchanged so much love in that moment that I was tripping, high as a kite. The next morning, I went to London, to Newham Hospital, for the last time. Her colors were green and gray before they switched all the different machines off. I took her hand and I started singing my medicine songs. For me, for her, for my sister and father, for every daughter that sent her mother safely to the other side. Nobody shushed me. There were nine other beds in that intensive care unit, lots of nurses and doctors, my dad never heard me sing before. None of it mattered. The machines were not beeping anymore, Mom's chest was no longer forced to move, my sister and dad were crying loud and my song carried all this energy to the place of stillness, back where it all came from.

So that's the story. I mean, this is a big story, I know. And even though I have no grudges, no unfinished business, no last words I wish I had said before she went, the gravity of the story itself is putting me in a kind of trance, a withdrawal from life, and closer to death. But the story is beautiful, it's one of forgiveness, love, finding freedom in an impossible relationship. Maybe that too is taking me closer to the veil. This whole experience… I can really appreciate the journey, you know? How I'm getting better and better at sitting with my feelings, resting with them. There is so much freedom in that space. And something else. Yes. A shamanic potential. Energy that is inviting me, enticing, welcoming. Ah, yes, now I understand why I needed to say this story out loud, so that I could come to my conclusions. Thank you, Edgar, thank you so much for being my friend and brother. It's so helpful. Just to know that you are there somewhere, listening, witnessing, holding the space for me. Thank you so much."

Feeling Love in the Face of Mass Destruction

Freya is the most beautiful woman I've ever met. All women I get to know well are beautiful, but there's something very special about her. Freya's physical appearance contains sadness and the deep wisdom of a young indigenous Native American dreamer as well as all magic, spontaneity and flirtatiousness of a mermaid. She gravitates men toward her like a black hole, and it's been both a blessing and a curse. She receives a lot of jealousy from women who often bond over their hostile feelings and thoughts about her. She also receives a lot of possessiveness from men who find their feelings irresistible and overwhelming. Rape attempts were unsuccessful only because of her fierce, wild nature and fearlessness when it comes to breaking free.

Freya is my cherished sister and teacher; she showed

me it's possible to feel love in the face of mass destruction caused by anger and rage.

We've traveled together many times – many pilgrimages, many countries and communities, alone in the woods, walking the mountains, sitting around the fire, in tipis, in sweat lodges, dancing, meditating. We've connected deeply with our waters; flowing freely like brisk ribbons of the mountain rivers, holding silent magic like the still Scottish lochs, tapping into the wild power of the crushing waves in the Caribbean Sea... Praying together for love, for freedom, for humanity, and for Mother Earth. Together, we've dared to go far in the embodiment of the wild feminine. No anchor, no looking back, no safety net. I had her back and she had mine. We've ventured way beyond anything we knew, shining the light of awareness in the deepest darkest corners of the feminine, and from there we were singing songs, weaving prayers, shining a smile of embodied knowing.

When Kiva[6] came to the UK, we knew we had to go. We packed the essentials in her unicorn campervan; cozy, soft, pink and blue. Just a little fluffy bedroom on wheels. And off we went to Oxfordshire to join two hundred other people who heard the calling to come together to Kiva – a vision of a Mexican medicine man – to pray for the Great Mother.

---

6 Kiva gathering is a ceremony of prayer for four days with indigenous elders and wisdom keepers from all across the world, with an intention to express gratitude to Mother Earth.

The place is magical. Open fields with the horizon so far and wide, it looks like a smile. This spaciousness enters your brain and lungs, inviting you to breathe slow and deep. Just landing there among the few canvas structures, with a tipi, prayer altar, high grass, smiling people, is magical enough. I feel home again. I feel okay, I see that people are okay and nature is okay. Walking around the Kiva grounds to familiarize ourselves with everything, people are giving us hugs and welcoming us so kindly that it feels like a long-awaited family reunion. I have a deep wish in my belly that one day, we will cohabit our green-blue planet in this beautiful way – together, in perpetual welcome. Maybe one day.

On the second morning at Kiva, the pow-wow drum is almost deafening. Twelve people drum in unison as people sing, rattle, pray with feathers. We're there, we know the songs. We join in, dancing as well. Medicine women are cleansing the space with cedar smoke, and everybody is slowly allowed in the main praying space, deeper in the earth, where we connect with ancient spirits, give our thanks, let Her know that we are here and we care. We feel her love, we hear her calling that we know what's happening and are active, that we take action to change the way humans live, that we already live our lives in a much more sustainable way, and slowly, that we invite others to do the same. Small steps. Love needs time. Love needs people to make their own decisions, invest in them. Like little seeds, they need nourishment, sunshine, water – you can't rush their growth. So does love in people's hearts. My body is shaking but my feet are sure as I dance around the altar singing my song, letting her know that I won't stop. I'll stay on my path of self-inquiry, meditation, stillness, and love. And I will keep planting seeds everywhere I go. I see many elders around me – they came from North and South America, Africa, the Middle East, from various different tribes. They are planting seeds too. Being so close to them is so nourishing to me. One smile and my whole being turns into white fluff blown away by the wind, like a dandelion. The locality called Aya disappears; there is now one rhythm of the pow-wow drum, one song, a circular vortex of energy. I give in to all of it and I go a whole level deeper.

Later that day, after the communal grazing around lunch time, we gather again to listen to the elders talking and to sing some more. There's this man I like so much. I noticed him the first day. His smile is so nice that it pours hot chocolate over my heart and does something funny to my knees. I feel all soft and gooey. I want to giggle and twirl around in circles. Honestly, if I had a tail, I would be wagging the shit out of it. It's outrageous what the presence of this guy is doing to me. I can't stop fantasizing about him, and I do it out loud to Freya whenever we have a moment alone. On our way to the toilet, to the van, in the van, on our way back, changing clothes, going for a cup of tea… I just keep telling her the details of how I would celebrate this man, how I would open to him like one thousand different flowers at different times of the day. And guess what, right now, singing songs, he's smiling back at me and I feel we have a connection. Sex is forbidden for the duration of Kiva, but it's so nice to just be in this space with him, bathe in the tingling vibrations of our connection. Soon we hug and keep singing the old songs together, embracing the delicious intensity of the moment. Freya is smiling so happily; she's joining the hug and we're all in this together. I'm filled to the brim of my awareness with joy. But after a while, I start noticing that she's flirting with him, gazing at him with her beautiful smile, touching him softly. A sting of jealousy brings poison to my thoughts. I decide to override this.

Look at me, I'm so ridiculous, I'm insanely in love with this guy and so possessive, this is making me paranoid and I'm seeing things that aren't there. It's just because she's so beautiful, I'm reading too much from this situation and will stop this nonsense immediately.

And I do. This is my superpower. I got it from growing up with alcoholic parents in a dysfunctional family. You learn to switch your feelings off to survive – it's necessary. It's not that much of a superpower, really. More of a problem, because feelings really shouldn't be ignored or numbed, ever. Anyway. I decide, using my reasoning, that it can't be what I'm reading, and I let it be. In fact, I leave them alone as a sign of my complete trust. I walk off and join the group of women sharing stories about their experience of being born as indigenous Native Americans, being uprooted, taken away from their tribes to white boarding schools, being indoctrinated and converted. They say that as a result, they don't belong anywhere; white people judge them by the indigenous features, their biological families don't recognize them because of the haunting gap in their belief systems and language. Outcasts wherever they go. These women find the courage to shine their tiny selves and transform their oppressive circumstances into advantages. First though, they hit rock bottom. They swim in the murky waters at the bottom of the collective shadow. They go through so much pain, darkness, self-hatred, isolation. Many of them have an intimate relationship with suicide. But when they come out on the other side, they are powerful beyond anything you've seen. They shine their vulnerability with courage. And they make a big difference in the world. I cry listening to their stories. They're so moving. They trust their feelings so much. I want to be like them.

I spend the whole day being inspired and moved. I am a social butterfly; I sing, drum, dance, meet people. It's beautiful. When I'm back in the van, it's so late and I'm so tired that I fall asleep almost instantly, held by the fairy lights in the shape of cute fluffy alpacas. Freya isn't there, and I think she must be having a great time too. I wake up in the morning and Freya's still not here. *Where is she?* And then I see her coming, wearing his shirt. It's white linen with embroidered red and yellow flowers and Mexican geometrical designs. My heart is broken. I feel betrayed. An ocean of tears blinds me. My whole body is shaken by rage. But I refuse to feel those feelings. This is such a beautiful place, I received so much kindness, experienced so much connection. Also, I don't want to be another jealous woman on Freya's path – no, not me. So I fight it. This creates an enormous tension. I withdraw from all aspects of the gathering. I avoid people. I don't talk to anyone, including Freya. I keep swallowing my tears. I can't really open my mouth, because the only thing that wants to come out is anger. I feel so deeply wounded, raging, alone. I feel there is no space here for my darkness.

After sunset, everybody gathers around a big bonfire. It's time for medicine plants with the Blue Lions. They are a band of Sikh warriors belonging to the ancient lineage of the warrior Akali Nihang Singhs. They have such a powerful presence. Everybody's there. Freya shares her sheepskin with the Mexican, inviting me to join them. I'm still in so much pain, my wounds bleeding silent tears. People are getting ready and we're just about to start. I feel I cannot take the medicine in this state. The bubbling cauldron of feelings is strong enough – if I add anything on top, it will be a disaster. So at the last minute, I leave. I go back to the unicorn van and cry myself to sleep in the soft embrace of the fairy alpaca lights. The tears are still there in the morning – for missing out, not being part of the community, the sense of injustice, suffering in silence, isolation. I'm so conflicted, wanting to be joyful in this happy place of Kiva.

Freya walks toward me with an innocent smile. She's high on connection with people, with fire, nature, and the whole of existence. I am pure rage. I hate her, I hate myself, and I hate this oppressively positive space. I'm completely lost in a deep dark hole. She tells me she would like to take time with me and the tobacco. She says she can sense something is off and she doesn't like it. I have tears in my eyes, unable to speak. She digs her rapé from the depths of the unicorn van and looks at me. Yes, I would like to sit with her. Unable to speak, I nod.

Rapé is a sacred medicine prepared by people in the Amazonian forest. It's a mix of dried and powdered tobacco and medicinal plants snuff, carefully put together to heal and give us strength. All indigenous people in North and South America have a lot of respect for tobacco. They heal with it, pray with it, cleanse with it, ask for guidance with it, journey with it… it's the most powerful plant. They say the spirit of tobacco is far too big for our tiny lungs, and that's why we get ill if we inhale it. I used to be a dedicated smoker, just loved my breaks at work for a quick smoke, loved the mingling with other smokers, and the coffee cigarette combo… oh my God, isn't that just the most satisfying form of a time-out?

But when I started developing my personal relationship with this medicine plant, I was quickly assured that inhaling is not a good way to go, and I stopped. No drama, no withdrawal symptoms, no putting on weight… I have a lot of respect and love for this plant. Just as almost everything else in life, tobacco is not what I learned when growing up. Sex is not what I saw in the movies or porn, not the real, juicy, passionate, fulfilling tantric stuff anyway. Relationships, money, God, community, vulnerability, strength, confidence, being of service, communication, illness, health, shamanism… almost nothing is what I thought back then.

Anyway.

Freya sits in front of me, our knees touching. She places a little of the powder on the palm of her hand and puts it in her blowpipe. She says her blessing for me out loud. Her heart is pure and the intention is beautiful. I welcome the medicine in – it feels like it's going directly to my head. I sneeze. There's a tingling sensation, carving out a little free space in my crowded mind. Just enough space to realize that I can't blow the medicine in her nose with anger. I can't. I look at her. I see her shiny eyes, her smile, her tattoos. I see something else. No, I don't see it with my eyes, I feel it. But it's like seeing. I realize that I love her so much. I take a deep breath in, and the feeling spreads. I'm connected with her again. It feels like I'm in the eye of the storm. It's completely silent here, with rage, anger, pain, all those feelings circling violently around. But the center is still. This is my bridge. I relax into this feeling. I say my blessing and blow the medicine in her nostrils with love. I have a tingling sensation all over my body. The overwhelming dark shadow is lifted. I want to tell her about my feelings, and we end up having a long conversation about sisterhood, old traumas, freedom. Turned out it was a healing experience for both of us.

Feeling love in the face of mass destruction. A priceless experience. Light and dark, love and hate, existing equally and at the same time. The ability to dwell there for a moment. This is a place of true power. You don't know what's possible until you're there, creating the new frontier. And then, with time, if you want, it becomes the new standard, the new "normal". But the magic of the moment, the potent energy, will always be there – you can tap into it anytime. Or you can completely let go of it, head toward new adventures, following the invitation of the heart, a birdsong, or anything else that calls you.

Sisterhood can be such an amazing thing. And it can happen in unexpected and mysterious ways. All we need to do is open up for it, and we'll get it.

One of my beautiful sisters, a friend and teacher, is a witch from Glastonbury. One morning, I felt a particular pull to go to Glastonbury. I wanted to get the water from the white and red spring to make a new batch of water kefir. I arrived early, filled my bottles, and took my dog up to the Tor. The winds on the top of that hill are so violent. They're very penetrating and transformative, if you allow them to be.

They say there is a portal on this hill. Many people pilgrimage here in search of a spiritual experience. For me, it's all in the wind.

There's a common misconception that all spiritual experiences are ecstatic and pleasurable. Some are, yes. But most times, they are uncomfortable, scary, painful, lonely, crazy. If people knew just how much they would suffer on this path, they wouldn't take it. They would put yellow tape around the entrance with big red warning signs. And that's how it was, back in the day. Only a small group of witches, druids, shamans, and sorcerers were initiated in that path, and not because they desired to do so. Times have changed though. Awakening retreats sell like fresh donuts. And they're so nice too – it's so much better to go through your shit surrounded by a lovely community.

We are walking up the Tor. My dog, Tryton, is a sheep hunter. When he finds one, he bullies it into submission in a very unskillful way. A few times, I was worried a farmer would appear with a gun and shoot him dead. They can do that in the UK, you know? It's scary. So I put him on a leash. It's better for the sheep and great for me – he is pulling me all the way up on the stone path. I'm on top of the hill, where the winds are at full power. I open my body to receive them. I'm so relaxed, shoulders down, breathing slow and deep. My hips and heart open, knees slightly bent, head in the center. And something else is relaxing deeply within the fabric of my being. I'm immediately covered in goosebumps, and I know that I'm receiving the energy of this place. A download and reset of my systems. I allow everything to happen, trying to maintain my silent mind. Breathing, feeling the tingling all over my body. I don't understand the significance of this moment – no voice, no visions, but a deep reassurance that all is well. There's no way of comprehending this intellectually, so it's best not waste my energy trying. Instead, I remain in deep meditation with no internal dialogue as I go back down the hill. I decide to have a dip in the freezing cold water of the White Spring. I leave my dog in the car and head toward the gate. It's shut; still fifteen minutes before public opening hours. I squat outside in silence, waiting for the gate to open, no one around. Suddenly, a woman emerges from the darkness of the cavern and says through the gate:

"I think you are here to help me, I felt your presence here very strongly. Do you want to come in?"

She has a sense of urgency about her, and her sentence is very matter-of-fact. I'm curious and want to help, so I say yes. I follow her to the big pool. It's dark, humid, and echoey. I shiver from the cold. Few candles are burning, and the only sounds are of water flowing. I can't pinpoint where the sounds come from – it feels like they're coming from everywhere. The floor of the cavern is wet and I can't see much in the darkness. The woman explains that she's here to let go of her unborn child she lost ten years ago. She says she feels ready to release and move on, but she is struggling with her process. She shakes slightly, very emotional. Her eyes pierce through me as she says:

"I'm ready to let go."

She goes in naked and I follow her in the same fashion. We stand knee-deep in the water. She's breathing heavily and the cavern echoes gently. After a moment, she starts singing her song. It's very animalistic, mourning and howling. Everything seems to be amplifying her voice and bringing the intention back to us; moist on the stone walls, candles, incense, the water running on the floor through the pools and altars, the small waterfall on the back wall of the cavern. Every particle around us and within us is saturated with the vibration of her grief. I'm deeply moved by all this. I stay with her. Present. Witnessing. Having trust that she knows what she's doing. I let her do her thing, in openness, in kind and compassionate presence. That's it. I hold her body, hold her pain and her song. She's shaking, crying. I feel a big release – some heaviness flowing down through my body, down to the waters. Silence. From the gentle sounds of the water around us emerges my song, a soothing lullaby. A nurturing melody of kindness. When that comes to an end, the woman takes time on her own at one of the altars, lighting a candle and connecting with her prayer, setting intention for what's to come next. I smudge the whole place with frankincense resin I bought on the local High Street just a couple of hours earlier.

We spend the whole day together, sharing stories of healing, relationships, traveling, exploring the spiritual world. We giggle a lot. She teaches me clairvoyance and I'm amazed just how easy it is. She tells me she always had a strong connection with the unseen world and has always been a bit of an outcast for it. Navigating the unseen world has always been easier than communicating with people. Now she's learning to accept her power and use it in a way that can be accepted and understood by others.

We're still in touch today, keep exchanging stories and support, holding space for each other. We're an inspiration and understanding for one another. It's so beautiful to be connected and bonded in the unseen world. No comparison, no judgment, no necessity for diplomacy, pleasantries or 'shoulds'. We see each other naked, beyond skin and bones. Every witch needs such a connection.

Months later, after my return from India, I decide to go to Glastonbury for a deep cleanse in the spring. I meet with her afterward. She takes a good look at me and tells me I look horrible.

"Oh, thanks."

"You are dehydrated and your liver is bad."

"Yes, I just came out of severe four-day diarrhea, that could be it."

She tells me to take seven days off anything I'm doing:

"Whatever you think you have to do right now, put it for later, cancel appointments, the world is not going to stop spinning without you doing stuff, this is important. And no planning, no figuring out, no organizing, no budgeting… nothing! Time off everything. Whenever you get a thought you need to do something, stop, just stop! Pick it up in seven days."

I do what she says. Almost. I smuggled in a bit of planning – send a few requests to join healing teams at festivals later that summer. Hardly any work. By the end of my seven days, I'm rested, my mind calm. Finally, I settle back into Bristol after coming home from India. And I settle back into my body too. And then I realize something. It had always been right in front of my face, for at least the last three years, after my pilgrimage in Colombia. I knew it all along; I was just too stubborn chasing dreams.

In Colombia, we were all taken to meet the elders, deep in the forest that covers the Sierra Nevada de Santa Marta. I was so happy.

Finally! I'm going to meet a tribe that carries old traditions, that isn't infected by the maladies of modern times, with a strong group of elders who know, who live in harmony with nature and each other, aligned, connected, calm, and clear. Finally, I get to understand the deepest secrets of existence, hidden like a gem in this mountain range.

I know, I was under a spell of Indiana Jones, and of course I internalized him; I had a mini Indiana in me, brave and willing to do anything to get to the holy grail. I was very excited and open to receive the wisdom. I had my gifts prepared to exchange with the elders. Humbled and grateful, excited to the brim of my unwavering smile, I chose a fern-infused oil that I'd made the previous autumn, the same one I used to heal arthritis pain with a lot of success with my clients. I thought it would be nice to show them that our wisdom and connection with plants in Europe isn't dead, you know?

When we arrived, we were welcomed so kindly and instantly became part of their family. The hospitality, curiosity, kindness, and generosity were absolute and so nourishing. It was insane. We sat for long hours around the fire. We asked a few questions, they spoke long and slow. Then we brewed chicha together – a traditional fermented drink. We all took turns to stir it, sing the special chicha song, dance around the cauldron in celebration, in trance. Suddenly, it was all done, and we sat on the dirt floor in the maloca, but the air was still moving around the fire in a circular way and I could hear an echo of our song coming from people's faces. One bowl. We all took a small sip and passed it on, sharing and drinking as one. That's when it first hit me. This was the big secret. What matters most in life is kindness, being a loving and welcoming family for each other, sharing, working, and celebrating together as one. This was the most precious wisdom there is. And it's so simple that it's overlooked and belittled. I wasn't expecting that at all. I was waiting for some grand vision of extraterrestrial life forms maybe, or a space-time portal between sky and the Earth, or any other extraordinary kind of magic. None of that. Just celebrating life together as one. And even though this realization hit me really hard and my heart was physically aching in open joy, I instantly dismissed it, forgot it. Moments later, one of the peeps was almost bitten by a deadly spider, someone else shared their psychedelic journey from the ceremony, and the wisdom I received disappeared completely, dissolved in the ocean of my desires – desires for peak experiences, for amazing adventures beyond ordinary life. Surely there was more to life than simply being together in a genuine, caring, beautiful way.

Really?

Awakening is a Deadly Business

My feet are buried in the sand. The sun is halfway down, bowing to the horizon. There's a red and blue cockerel painted skillfully on the table, folk-style, with defined lines and single-tone fillings. The beak is open, suggesting a *cock-a-doodle-doo*, but the only sound is of the wind and waves crashing on the beach. Tall coconut trees sway around me. The horizon is inviting me to be open and spacious with my thoughts. I realize while writing this book that I've been stalling about telling one story in particular – perhaps the cornerstone of my journey, the reason I'm writing in the first place. The story of my time with Kirt – a dramatic and transformational time that finally led me to total freedom and unconditional love.

Creating the Holy Cunt is such a deep meditation for me. Shamanic too. I start each swriting ession by relaxing fully, here and now; everything planned for later can wait, everything that was stays in the past. Slowly, my mind goes into a state of no thought. In that emptiness, I bring my intention, pure and strong, to write my story in a beautiful, inspiring way. Intention is so important. And then I simply allow the words to flow through me, just as they want. As they flow, I re-live the moments, discovering hidden gems and having "aha!" moments.

How far will I dare to go describing the events with Kirt? Is it even possible to relax and sustain the state of hollowness while recollecting what had happened? The story is still reverberating, still sore in my body, my heart. Do I really want to re-live those painful moments?

I don't. That's why I've been stalling.

For a moment, I do nothing, just allow all these thoughts to be. They eventually fade away, and now there are only feelings and bodily sensations; tingling under my skin, something crowded in my belly, a little tightness in my head. These sensations, with no story attached to them, are actually quite nice. So much aliveness is happening within me right now. I smile to myself. This aliveness is helping me to move on, let go of the pain, notice there are other feelings present as well. The cockerel on my table is still making his silent noise. My toes are playing in the white sand. Suddenly, I hear some nice instrumental music on the speakers in the restaurant, and this gives me the final push to shift my mood.

It had all started with a vision. Vast spaciousness with no color. And in that spaciousness – no light, no shadow, no time, no wind – a fluorescent light; pink and green, dancing together in form of two long bodies with hundreds of legs, twirling and moving around each other mesmerizingly… yes, that was the beginning. It was so innocent.

What would happen if you could relax completely into the totality of your being?

Relax completely into your feet, spine, liver, jaws, belly. Then relax into your feelings, thoughts, and bodily sensations. Relax fully into the space that you occupy with your physicality and your energy. Relax your desires, your plans, your previous achievements and failures. Just a soft *yes* to everything that is right now, including what you can see, smell, feel, and touch.

That's how I felt with Kirt, my guru and tantra teacher, when he was around. Softness and easiness, and so much spaciousness I felt like an astronaut, even between my thoughts. There was nothing I wanted or needed to do – just a lot of potential, like the bubbling surface of a volcano, red-hot lava resting, simmering softly at the bottom of a crater, yet ready to explode any moment, covering miles and miles around it in liquid fire, molten rock, ash, steam. You can imagine just how much I was hooked to that peak experience that was present nonstop when sharing my time-space with my guru. I wanted to drink it, bathe in it, dance it, stretch throughout the full length of it. I loved being on the edge, sensing this current of potential while being in ultimate stillness with my feelings, absolutely relaxed and at ease. I was so excited about where it might take me. I was like Alice in Wonderland, curiously exploring entire new dimensions.

Kirt knew what this potential was capable of. He felt it too. He said this energy would open a portal, an opening we would both jump through. What was going to happen when we jumped, nobody could say for sure. Perhaps we would never come back to this reality, perhaps we would manifest a new world. But he had a plan. He was very happy to meet me – said I was the most awakened person he'd met in his life, that we were the ones to wake up the world. That's how powerful the space between us felt. All we needed to do was surrender, dive in fully, go for it without any remorse or looking back, all systems go. I was excited beyond anything I knew.

Yeah, I mean, I know surrender, it's been my mantra for over a year now, I've been practicing. And my whole life is just one courageous dive after another – I can do this.

Everything made total sense in my mind. All my life had brought me to this moment. I saw clearly how it was a blessing to go through all that darkness and abuse early in my life. I embraced it, forgave my villains, opened my heart fully to experience love and joy, with all the fierce courage and fearlessness of a honey badger. I was restless on my journey, in seeking out unlimited freedom and unconditional love, shedding layers and layers of conditioning, limitations, ancestral trauma… I knew beyond a shadow of a doubt that I'd been clearing a path for what was going to happen with Kirt! And I trusted this man. I had known him for almost a year now. We spoke every day. He was kind, sweet, caring, smart, funny. He loved me and accepted me all the way, with every quirk of my nature. He encouraged me to be more – more of everything that was true and honest within me. And so I was. My love for him developed into such a strong fire, the alchemy of this relationship, that even though it was just via WhatsApp, he shone like a sun in my life, inviting me to soften, to open up even more, to trust and surrender, to sing the songs of wildfire within me. And I did. I kept unfolding and diving within myself, enveloped in a vast, funny, loving, sexy welcome from Kirt.

At that time, he was already in India. He came there from Madeira where he'd spent the previous couple of years. Before that, he was in Los Angeles, before that, Romania, before that… who knows. Now it was time for India. Since we were in constant conversation via WhatsApp, he knew I had quit my job, and with the little savings I had, it was time for me to explore India too. Various people had often asked me about my experience in India, like it was my second home that I went regularly back to. When I'd say I had never been, they would be surprised and often said I should go.

So finally, I went. Two weeks in South Goa, on my

own. Beautiful and simple. A little hut in a garden, lots of other female solo travelers from over the world. Delicious, juicy fruits for breakfast, coffee and talks – exchanging life stories and tips for shopping, sightseeing, yoga practice, giggles. I learned how to deal with mosquitoes and now they rarely bite. I learned how to communicate with shopkeepers from Rajasthan and Kashmir, and they too were friendly, just sad that I wasn't buying. I talked to business owners on the beach, who complained there weren't enough tourists. The regular tourists would say it was the same amount of them, but the number of shops and bars was growing ridiculously.

"They don't think. They see their neighbor doing well with his business and they open exactly the same one next door. Most bars on this beach have exactly the same menu. I remember this beach when there were just two bars. Now there's twenty. It's nobody's fault, really. It's funny though."

I spoke to Indian men about this and they blamed their wives for being too greedy, telling me about how they keep complaining that they should earn more money. I spoke to Indian women, who complained that the men were lazy. Both Indian men and women complained about tourists for not spending more money on their services. There were no winners here, and I left it be.

Having seen most of South Goa, I decide to go north. I know Kirt is there, so I arrange to meet him. He's very happy and eager to meet; he negotiated a discount for me in the resort he's staying in. It's so nice of him, especially since he's staying in a place way above my usual budget. I was thinking I would rent something cheaper in the area and just meet him elsewhere. I'm humble and easygoing, so you know, no problem. But here I am, in a taxi, heading toward luxury. Two hours to go. We're halfway through the journey. The taxi driver, also arranged by Kirt, is really nice. He's wearing white corporate clothes and I think I must be going to a different world now. But the roads are still very dusty and cows shit everywhere. Nah, same old. I send Kirt a video clip from the car, I'm so excited. I haven't got any plans in particular, but the last two times we've met, it was just so awesome. We made music together, giggled loads, sunbathed naked in a meadow, talked, talked, talked. It's just so easy with him, and so magical. I keep smiling to myself, sometimes out loud. The taxi driver is kind and stays focused on the road. He let me put my playlist from YouTube on the speakers. Suddenly, I get a message from Kirt asking to meet at LaMuella. He's very mysterious, didn't give me any more details. I ask the driver, who says it's very close to my destination of Mandala. He says okay, no problem. It's really nice that Kirt is making this special welcome party for me. I like the mysterious tone and can't smell anything fishy at all. I arrive at LaMuella and instantly like it. It has an expensive boutique at the front, with designer clothes from New Delhi and price tags from New York. Is it just for the wealthy Russian tourists? They buy these things and make it impossible for me to haggle the price. These shopkeepers don't want to sell loads of stuff.

They sell one garment and that's the equivalent of an annual waiter's salary in Bengaluru. Anyway, I still like it. I walk between the racks of clothes, and deeper into the space is the café, with big tables for communal eating and drinking in the middle – heavy wooden antique things. Each chair here is different, which makes it wonderfully chaotic, but somehow everything fits together nicely. The corners are all cozied up with large beds snuggled with cushions. You can lie in, sit, eat, drink, indulge in comfort, have a slow afternoon. Lots of white fabrics are floating in the draft, butterflies fly in and out through the open walls. I find a place to sit. He comes shortly after. We hug for a good ten minutes. No words; just this smushy presence of two, a little sweaty, together. We've been talking via WhatsApp so much that we've exchanged all the intellectual stuff many times over, but this physical presence is new. We sit down, positioning all the cushions behind the shoulders, arms, and lower back, gazing at each other and giggling. Smoothies are on their way. Yep, I'm on top of the world. This is the high life for me.

He keeps talking about lots of stuff and I take it all in without trying to follow the stories. I just bathe in the sound of his voice, his chest moving up and down, supporting his breathing. I'm enjoying this. Then, he suddenly comes to his point for calling this meeting at LaMuella.

"I didn't tell Dolina you were coming."

Dolina is his life companion. They live like husband and wife, sharing everything together. I've never actually met her, but I know she's a big part of his life.

"Why didn't you tell her?"

This is a bit odd. I really don't know why he wouldn't.

"Well, because she is so sensitive, and every time I receive a message from you, she has a fit of anger and has a bit of a reaction any time I mention your name."

Shit. Really?

But I don't break his monologue, so he continues:

"I wanted to tell her many times, but there was just no good time for this, so maybe, you know, we go now together, and say hello?"

I study his face for a moment and come to the conclusion that he's telling the truth.

I tell him:

"You are fucked."

He is. Completely and utterly. How doesn't he see it? She obviously has an allergy to me and I'm the last person she wants to share space with. And she's no fairytale princess – more a confrontational, angry, fire-breathing dragon kind of woman.

He looks at me with an innocent smile.

"What do you mean, 'I'm fucked?'"

But I see that he knows. He knows he's fucked, he just doesn't realize the full extent of the situation, so I entertain him by stating the obvious:

"Obviously, she doesn't like my presence in your life as it is, from a distance, via WhatsApp, and now I will live here full time, in a hut next to yours. And you kept it a secret. You are fucked."

His face changes as I speak these words. It's not even what I say. It's how I say it. With an impending sense of doom. He understands. I see a little boy who just found out that the Christmas tree he destroyed means there will be no Santa this year. I'm very serious, but I also want to laugh.

Such a smart guy. He's had more lovers than I can count. Surely, he would know women by now?

Maybe he does know. Maybe he was just delaying the inevitable and was hoping that somehow, I'd show up and weave my magic on her.

Well. This is not my shit. I'm not going to take responsibility for it, thank you.

But I love him very much, every little bit of his soft tissue. So I put my stories and feelings aside and give him all my compassion. This guy is going down between the two women he loves the most in the entire universe. It's going to hurt.

I like this idea of four main archetypes that build women's psyche: the maiden, the mother, the enchantress, and the crone. It's all there – sometimes we identify with one more than the other, sometimes some archetypes are not mature, sometimes we use them to do bad things – but it's all there. They move with the tides of our menstrual cycles, with the life cycles and with other cycles too. They can also help us on demand. For example, we could be a very nurturing and caring mother in a relationship with someone, and very neglecting, narcissistic, and demanding with someone else.

The maiden is young, naive, fragile, and sensitive. She doesn't know, but she's open to exploring and learning for the sake and fun of doing it. She falls in love, has big dreams, sings with the birds, etc. Guess what the dark side of the maiden is. I'll leave it there. We all see it every day anyway.

The slut is my favorite archetype. She's also called the enchantress. I went to a solstice ceremony recently, and the pagan witch who facilitated the space didn't mention her. She's not mentioned in general. She's been the troublemaker in the history of humanity, so the tendency is to throw her away, deny her, give her an abusive label, chain her, burn her... but when you work on self-love, when you develop a deeply nourishing relationship with yourself, the enchantress blossoms and is capable of magic! I'm telling you, it's worth the trouble.

But here we come to the crone. The wise woman. The

One Who Knows. This is what came out for Kirt at LaMuella. I tell him everything he needs to know – about women, about relationships, about communication. I don't do it in a fluffy way, don't use any metaphors, don't paint beautiful pictures with my words to describe the landscape of this terrain. Just convey the message in a simple and straightforward way so that his shocked body and mind can absorb it. He gets it. He takes a moment to recompose himself to face Dolina, and off he goes. I order a soda and settle into my bewilderment for a moment. I refuse to make sense of it. If I'd taken the time and effort to see this man for who he was, maybe none of the things that followed would have happened. But then I wouldn't be telling my story to you now.

One last sip of lime soda with guilty sugar and off I go to Mandala to check in.

I'm kindly welcomed by the staff. They know about my arrival and show me around. My hut is literally next door to Kirt's. I smile and take my key. The walls are made of woven coconut leaves, certainly no barrier for sound. They also let some sun in. The wind rustles the leaves of my roof ever so gently. The hut is just big enough for a giant bed and a rail for clothes. There's a floor fan and a bedside table with a lamp. It's very simple and very nice, I love it. I feel a bit uneasy about the hut next door.

What's happening with Kirt and Dolina?

I don't really want to think about it. I take a towel and

spend the evening on the beach alone, connecting intimately with the sunset and the sea.

North or South Goa, the Arabic sea has the same breeze, the same sand. I find the tiny little stretch of the nudist beach and take my clothes off. Then I put them back on again. There's something about India that keeps me from relaxing in a public space with no clothes. Only once so far have I spent a good chunk of time naked on the beach.

It's a beach tucked away, with nobody on it – one of the beaches marked as a nature reserve to allow the turtles to come and lay eggs. No bars, no tourists. Hawks sit on the high branches of the surrounding trees, diving for the kill every now and then. In the company of the wild birds and howling winds, I take my clothes off and open my legs to receive the sunset. At first, I notice the gentle caressing of my skin. It's like being kissed by a thousand lips. My skin is tickled, my hair attentive to receiving the sweet whispers. The wind is soft and warm. Tiny grains of sand circulate curiously around the hills of my body, landing gently on my skin, rolling down the sun-kissed landmarks, making new homes in the valleys around my collarbones, elbows, breasts.

The gentlest of sensations, yet so profound, they bring such a sweet pleasure of being completely embodied, in the moment. I notice I'm breathing deeper, my belly moving up and down with excitement. The crushing of the waves, the wind, the cry of the birds. They are all inviting me to open. I surrender more and more, saturating myself in the sounds, allowing myself to receive the touch of the sand and wind. I hear a song in my heart. I listen carefully and then sing with it. Tears of joy flood my eyes, rolling down my ears, lips, wetting the sand below. I keep moving my body to the invisible tender rhythm of the moment. I keep singing with tears in my throat. The song changes slightly with rhythm and tempo. The golden light is delivered to me on the glowing tops of the waves, crashing hard on the flat surface of the wet sand one by one. With every wave, I feel the energy enter my body and gather, increasing in my navel. My skin stretches, my throat expands to the horizon, the energy in my womb reaches my heart, and I climax.

I look around. Not a single human in sight. It's so serene. And, yes, that just did happen. I shrug in a giggle. An explosion of energy that happened between me and the elements. That's a first. I feel I'm being held and looked after, and I rest and surrender in that.

I smile at this memory. No, not today.

Kirt sends me a message saying that Dolina took it very badly. I let it in and let it go. I sing to the moon and feel she is listening. The wind is soft and kind. The glistening waves find their way straight into my mind, keeping it calm. I'm in no hurry. Just sitting on the sand in suspension.

The moon, the sea, the wind… they were all listening, they were with me attentively like best friends. Silently. If only I had asked a question, they would have revealed everything to me. But I didn't want to know. The witch in me was still awakening, and she needed to experience what was coming.

Back at the reception in Mandala, I sign up for early morning yoga practice and go to sleep. I can hear the sea waves from my pillow, singing gentle lullabies as I disappear into the darkness of my closed eyelids.

Mandala is such an amazing place to be. Settled in a garden with plenty of open space to enjoy the sun, shade, hammocks, beds… everything's here. The yoga session is great. We're all gathered in a moon-shaped patio between the overgrown banks of a river and a big Ganesha statue. Burning incense keeps the early morning mosquitoes away. There is no wind. The sun lurks through the trees, kissing us good morning. Everybody is breathing deeply and flowing from one posture to another. So serene. Halfway through the session, we all hear a roaring kind of sound. Something like:

"Nooooooooo..!"

It's animalistic, vicious. We all look at each other, chills down our spines. We stop for a moment.

Are they okay down there?

Enkeli, the yoga teacher, smiles and invites us to continue with the asana. We carry on, hoping the world outside our practice will take care of itself for the time being.

The session finishes and I feel like staying on my mat, chanting the Ganesha mantra. Everybody leaves and I do just that for a while. I feel at peace. There is just the vibration of my voice. Everything else dissolves into nothingness; it's so nice to be in this space – my own personal garden in the space of awareness. I finish with an overwhelming feeling of gratitude and... hunger. My stomach is just so empty. I didn't have dinner or supper last night. It's definitely breakfast time. I find the restaurant and see Enkeli, some of the resort staff, and Kirt all gathered together around a table. I fill my plate with fresh fruits and join them. They tell me things are not good. It was Dolina who sounded the roar. She punched Kirt in his stomach and smashed his phone.

"What? Why?"

He told her yesterday that I was in Goa. But she was so upset to know I was in the same province that he couldn't find it in him to tell her I was in the same village, the same resort… they woke up this morning and, as they came to the restaurant for breakfast, the staff told them that their friend, Aya, had a good night's sleep and was already out and about. They were being nice, they were informed we were good friends. And in that moment, she lost it. I'm surprised that Kirt is sharing his life with such a volatile human being.

I mean, what the fuck… we're just friends, nothing ever happened between us, not even a kiss.

They tell me that after she punched and cried, she stormed into my hut, then walked all around Mandala threatening to kill me.

Wow.

I ask Kirt if she has it in her to hurt me and he just looks at me.

Fuck. I really believed I was protected by forces much greater than her fury. She didn't find me at yoga practice, so I get to live, but for how long?

I'm being told she's looking for me at the beach now. I continue with my breakfast, not so much out of hunger as the fact that it might be my last meal, so I want to enjoy it. I laugh to myself and tell them what I'm thinking. We all giggle, trying to release the tension. When she comes back, her face is red. Her body smells of sweat. She looks like she's ready to kill.

Fuck.

She puts her face close to mine, sticks a finger right in my nose, and shouts at me directly from the raging fire in her belly. She tells me to get the fuck away from her, because she will punch me in my face. I look at Kirt. He nods. Okay. Clearly, this is not a good time to discuss or reason things out. I don't want her to punch me. Kirt is…

who knows what he is. So I get up and go in silence. She shouts abusive stuff at my back as I walk away.

Back in my hut, my hands are shaking and my heart is beating wildly. My body is in survival mode. I feel a lot of energy, like I could go running for hours on end. I pack a beach towel and choose to go for a swim instead. I'm disappointed and shocked. I hadn't expected anything like this. On my way out, she yells more abusive lines toward me from the porch of her hut. I feel adrenaline building in my muscles but choose not to react. The staff are very polite and smile at me. They have no idea. I have no idea either. I shrug my shoulders at them and just go.

Being on my own is soothing. I hide nothing. I can be with myself, just as I am, with everything. No excuses, no explanations. So I take time to lick my wounds, I listen to my complaints and what-the-fucks. At the end of the day, a decision grows in me to stay at Mandala. I don't know why. It just feels good to stay. But I know to trust my gut instincts, and in any case, I don't want to run away in fear. I actually had a rather good day; I enjoyed the sea, the beach, the sun. On my way back to Mandala, I pause at the Ashiyana yoga retreat center. They have an amazing Shala, a massive structure made of heavy dark wood. A beautiful altar. White mosquito nets instead of walls. Crickets and frogs living in the thick foliage around it orchestrate a beautiful symphony. It's empty at the moment – it must be in-between yoga sessions. I go in, take all my clothes off, and in the semi-darkness of just a couple of candles, do my yoga practice. Just a few poses held with long and deep breathing. I'm left undisturbed for an hour and a half. I am calm, serene, and my body feels great, stretched and oxygenated. I'm ready to go back to Mandala, albeit not sure what to expect.

Will I die tonight?

No messages from Kirt. I don't feel like confronting the dragon, so I just walk silently in the protection of the night. I light a candle next to my bed. I'm scared again.

Is she going to come and kill me in my sleep? Maybe it would be safer to sleep on the beach tonight?

But I don't want to sleep on the beach. And I refuse to be a scared little victim. Something very old and wild in me is taking charge. I see myself cutting my skin open and dripping blood. I take a feather and a rattle. I make a circle around my bed, write protective runes on it, and seal it with the vibrations of my voice and my rattle. The feather takes my prayer out and up.

I'll be safe tonight. I can go to sleep. But will I? I had a good life. I did the best I could, always. No regrets and no disappointments. But I want to live a little longer – yes, I like the crazy adventures of being alive. But at the same time, if it's my time to go, it's my time to go. Surrender.

I wake up in the morning. I'm so glad to be alive. The early sun makes its way through the little grid of coconut leaves weaved around the walls of my hut, planting little dots of light on my duvet, pillow, skin. I take a deep inhale, inviting the light in with my breath. I play with the little dots for a moment in silence, moving my hands, arms, exposing my belly to the dancing spots of light. I love my body so much. I love to experience the warmth, the colors, the scents, the sounds... I can't hear anything outdoors. Just early morning birds and insects. Everybody must be still sleeping. Then I notice that I'm focusing on the hut next to me;

Am I trying to hear Dolina?

Abruptly, the tranquil moment changes to one of complete terror. Fear of being bullied, harassed publicly, maybe punched.

What's waiting for me today?

I have a moment of wonder and humor that I live in this world of duality, moving from being profoundly happy and at peace to completely consumed by fear.

Is this why I want to live? This insane mad mix of feelings?

I allow it to be for a moment. All feelings and thoughts, just letting them be as they are, no need to change or fix them. After a while, the sensations ease and my body stops trembling.

Okay then, Hoka Hey, let's do this.

I take a breath in and step outside my hut.

The fire-breathing dragon is nowhere in sight, and I have my yoga and breakfast in peace, only a gentle shadow of fear shadowing it. People came to ask me how I am. Everybody likes a bit of drama, and people are curious and kind. We share our bewilderment. We laugh and connect. I feel supported and feel my body eases just a bit.

Just as I'm thinking I could use a friend right now, I meet a German tourist who lost her luggage in transit. Insurance will pay for the new set of fashion items, how amazing is that. We spend the day looking for flip-flops, bikinis, tops, and shorts, exploring coffee shops and restaurants, sharing stories, listening to and supporting each other. Two strangers in need become best friends for a day, giving each other a helping hand to stand on their feet again. What a medicine, huh? I had a lovely day and didn't see or hear from Kirt or Dolina. I let them be. I feel much safer tonight. My feelings are still confused, and I'm still very much suspended in the explosion, curious to find out what's going to happen next.

I don't know it yet but this ability to sit with my fear is linking me directly to the Witch from my recurring childhood dream. Squatting on my heels, hugging myself close to my body in a dense cloud of petrifying fear – she's coming to get me and nothing is going to stop her. Yes, I'm still waiting. Not quite sure what's coming, but I'm maturing to face it now. I'm so tired. Every day, for the last ten years or so, there's always been a moment when I feel exhausted. I've been eliminating things from my diet, meditating more, taking care of myself more, loving myself more, stressing less… and I'm still exhausted. Well, now I know it was all due to my internal turmoil. Hiding from the Witch in tantalizing fear of being at the center of it.

Finally, on the third day, Dolina approaches me and says we need to talk.

"Okay."

We sit in a beautiful space, under the bodhi tree. The air isn't moving, no birds are singing. Everything is at a standstill. The outside is my inside. My inside is the outside. I am suspended and waiting. Silence, tension, but also calmness and quiet. The dragon speaks first. She tells me how cheeky I am to come here where they live now, to ruin their peaceful nest. How horrible for me to bring my insolent smile, to invade their personal space and shamelessly parade like nothing's going on. She tells me who I am and what I think. She tells me she can see through my fake facade. I am no love, I am full of shit. The words keep streaming from her mouth. Each one feels like an arrow. They attempt to pierce through the soft spots of my being. She then continues to tell me how I should change my behavior and my life view. I keep listening. My hands are shaking and I hold them together. Yes, I feel rage and fear, but there's something else emerging. A deep understanding is forming in my heart. The dragon is speaking about her fear and deep desire to control her environment in desperate search for safety. She doesn't know me, we never spoke before this moment. This is not about me at all. This is about her. And then something extraordinary happens. I see her. The real her. The beautiful, shining love wrapped tightly in pain, misfortune, and fear. I am flooded with compassion for her. My eyes fill with tears and I have to stop her. I explain what my feelings are. She stops. Looks at me differently. She says she's getting goosebumps. Then she cries. She says she doesn't want to like me, she hates me, but instead, she feels this love for me, and we both reach a deep understanding of this moment. Beyond language, beyond words or the ability for the human mind to understand reality in all its complexity. It doesn't make sense, but for now, that's all there is – just pure, free-flowing love. We both open to flow with it. In that moment, I gain insight; I can see both of us sitting with our longings, pain, fears, and desires. Different stories, same feelings. I also understand that my presence at Mandala has shone a light on something in their relationship that had been lurking in the darkness for a long time now, unaddressed, unwelcomed, uninvited, but persisting to be seen. I share this with her and I see that she knows it too. We both gain access to the deeper wisdom as we open to the totality of this intense moment. We still have our differences, but now there is a deeply-rooted respect for each other. When we part, I am spellbound, speechless and in awe of the miraculousness of life.

From this moment on, Kirt and Dolina will never be the same. The fourteen-year-old vision of their relationship had been flapping in the wind like a sun-bleached flag, out of sight, in the middle of nowhere. The change was inevitable. Her intuition was right, her world was coming to an end and she wasn't ready for it, so she put up a fight. An embodied Sekhmet, the fiercest female warrior and healer in Egyptian mythology. I was the catalyst. Because Kirt was feeling alive around me. Inspired, motivated, energized, horny. A mix she hadn't witnessed for a long time. But it was way too painful to look within. So she exploded on me. Sekhmet is said to be the protector of the pharaohs; she led them in warfare, even after she died. Dolina believed in Kirt – her lover, companion, guru, and spiritual teacher. She taught him tantra, nurturing and supporting him to the best of her abilities, and he closed up on her. So much grief. So many hopes that never came true. She had been putting up with his love affairs, mischiefs, and side-adventures… and what was she getting in return? Closing up on her more and more. That was the true story behind her dragon fire.

And I had needed this experience too. I needed to sit in the explosion of this. I needed to find the courage to stay. I desperately needed to stop hiding from the Witch. I needed to face the dragon and find a way to look her in her glowing red eyes, in stillness, in surrender. A true rite of passage. An initiation.

After this experience, I gave myself permission to rest. I ate well, bathed in the sea, spoke to strangers, danced, got massaged, smoothied, and coffied to the brim. Got myself a scooter and drove anywhere the wind took me. Indian traffic… well, I wasn't killed by the dragon, so I decided I wasn't going to die now! Yes, I was in paradise.

I spent the most beautiful time with a Native American DJ who served people the medicine of music through which to dance and connect. One of the most inspiring people I met in Goa, he told me he had been serving ayahuasca half his life, helping people to heal mentally and physically. In his opinion, music was the next stage for people to learn how to express themselves freely, explore freedom in movements, giving, receiving, and connecting with the miracle of life and each other. I couldn't have agreed with him more. He was a very skillful maestro, serving sounds and holding space for people to unfold in their intimacy, vulnerability, and hidden beauty.

I met some handpan drummers I wished I could unhear, massage therapists who needed to learn boundaries (*I gave them a lesson, hell yeah!),* clothing designers who showed me fabrics and cuts I'd never seen in my life, and singers who sang straight from the heavens, opening me so wildly to the mystery of love I thought I would break open and never come back as Aya.

Kirt and Dolina spent a lot of time talking and working on a new arrangement for being together. I never asked about that. But I madly enjoyed the little snippets of time I spent with Kirt. Everybody around us enjoyed it too; explosions of giggles, banter, wild stories. There was a lot of sexual energy in how we spoke, spaces between the words, sentences, even the way we laughed. Open sexuality, the unlimited welcome to bring yourself fully, be totally, playfulness, deep connection, the simple pleasure of being in each other's company, was a wild mix that people found irresistible. It rippled and splashed on every fabric of matter within a ten-meter radius. Everybody loved to be around us. We were so open and jolly, enjoying life so much that cheeks hurt from laughing. These were the little snippets that Kirt offered me alone. One hour today, two hours tomorrow.

Christmas Special

To my surprise, on Christmas Eve, Dolina and Kirt invite me to smoke Changa together. I'm shitting myself in fear. Literally – one hour solid on the toilet until my bowels are finally clear. Every time I go communicating with the spirits around Christmas time, it's extraordinarily powerful and scary. I never take a decision like this lightly.

However, fear never stops me from doing anything, and this is thanks to my father. It was a hard-earned blessing, but what a treasure! My dad was always angry, like the Hulk, just not as handsome as Mark Ruffalo. My dad was nearly always green, big, and smashing things. The smallest thing got me into trouble; his way of disciplining a child was beating them with a leather belt. He was the scariest thing in the world. Getting beaten up was so painful, I wasn't able to sit on my ass for a while after, wasn't able to hear or see what was happening around me. So much pain. The physical pain faded away quickly but the emotional shadow of fear built up and accumulated. Growing up, every journey back home until I was eighteen was filled with terror. I would ask myself endless questions:

Did I leave any piece of clothing anywhere outside my wardrobe? Did I vacuum well enough? Was today my day to do the washing up?

A thousand other little things that could get me in trouble were all examined while walking back home from school. My hands would sweat, my breath was short, my heart was pounding. I was shaking and trembling but still walking home one step at a time. After that kind of training, stretched over twelve plus years, fear will never stop me now. Thanks, Dad. I mean it.

I allow my bowels to open completely and fully in this bathroom with no roof, with a view of coconut trees and two white fluffy clouds, and I think it's a good thing:

At least I won't shit myself later with them two gurus.

Can you imagine Dolina helping me to clean my shit? I don't think so.

Midnight. Christmas Eve. We smoke Changa. I want to smoke but am not inhaling right. My hands are shaking. I'm wasting half the pipe load. Dolina takes it from me and shows me again how to do it. She takes it all in and off she goes, giggling in a fit of pleasure. Kirt smiles at her absent, resting body, and whispers to me:

"She always gets love when she uses psychedelics. I can't stop myself thinking that it's because she created this hell on Earth for herself. She has this impenetrable armor that is isolating her from everyone. She always expects the worst from people, and a lot of times she gets it. Self-perpetuating system. And the vicious circle closes with her direct confrontational comments, heavily blasted with her opinions. I'm so glad she is in heaven now. She is clearly in so much pleasure."

I look at her and look at him. I say nothing. What will I get? Soon enough, it's my turn to try again. Dolina's words are ringing in my ears:

You are full of shit, Aya.

Well, not at the moment, I'm not.

I take the tiny glass pipe and take a good inhale.

Hoka Hey.

I close my eyes and fall gently on the bed. My everyday awareness is still there – I know where I am and that I'm smoking Changa. In the darkness, many spheres move around me, each one spinning in a different direction and at a different speed. A sphere within a sphere within a sphere… like a Russian Matryoshka doll. For a moment, all the spheres align and create a tiny little opening. This chink is too small to go through. I can see some kind of Great Beyond through it, but there's no pull, no push, no movement to go, so I just look at it for a while until all the spheres and the opening disappear. Next, I'm immersed in beautiful neon geometry, fractals – all moving, fascinating, and beautiful. I remain aware of the fact I'm lying on the bed, and at some point, I decide to stop looking at the hypnotizing shapes and come back to Kirt and Dolina.

"Why do you think you were not able to go through the opening? Do you think you are not ready to go or was the dosage too small?"

Kirt is curious.

"I'm not sure, maybe it's both? I really don't know."

Like me, Kirt isn't too interested in the colorful displays of the geometrical designs. We're both hungry for what's beyond that. We agree to smoke again on Boxing Day. This time, I'm not afraid. This time, we're set up out in the open, under the starlit sky. I've been fasting for the whole day. I hear the insects and coconut trees around, whispering soothing notes. Tonight, I'm really looking forward to it, genuinely excited. What I don't know is that Kirt has increased the dosage dramatically – so much so that some people never come back. People have died in the past. Kirt is taking a risk here, as he knows that to go beyond the veil and not just watch the display of pretty patterns, you need to take that risk. He made that choice for all of us. And kept it a secret. Dolina goes first and is soaking again in the love and giggles. Her trip encourages me – it's all going to be fine. I smoke – all in – and am gone before I hit the bed.

I can't remember the first part. I only know there was something before as I start to regain an awareness of being somewhere without space. Everything is so condensed, and I'm part of this gigantic moving thing. No space for breath. No breath at all. No body. Only a movement of crushing forces, twirling in spirals, circles, orbits. I am the spirals and I am the movement. It feels like a massive willpower brings me back to my identity, back to thoughts and feelings I recognize as myself. The awareness of Aya makes a decision to live. My breath comes back, and I am so happy to be alive.

Kirt asks me how it was.

"You know the geometrical patterns that we saw before? I was the patterns. And guess what, I think there was a chance I could have stayed there, never come back. But something pulled me back, brought me back to my body. I think this time, I experienced the other side of the coin of life."

He tells me then about how he increased the dosage to a dangerous level – something he read in a book he was given before coming to India. I ask him:

"What would you do if I didn't come back?"

He says he knew I would. I have no more questions. I'm spaced out, trying to comprehend what just happened.

What was I doing sticking my fingernails into the cracks

of the veil?

Ah, that's my curiosity and longing. The very dangerous longing to reunite with being one with everything around me. To experience what's underneath the material existence. I know I could have died just now. I'm a little shaken. I'm also reconnected with the purpose of life itself. I want to be here and now, in this body, under these coconut trees, surrounded by the noise-making insects and these two crazy astronauts, Kirt and Dolina. I'm not angry at him for giving me a potentially deadly dosage of Changa. I know it would be normal to be angry. It would be an acceptable reaction to cry or yell at him for making such a decision for me. But I also know my yearning to know. It's like a black hole. I can't not go there. I'm restless.

All the key moments I've experienced in my life have led me to this. Every relationship, my upbringing, all the healing, yoga, meditation, ecstatic dance, tantra, the moments of awakening, every near-death experience, sitting all night around the fire… I've followed the breadcrumbs to release the heavy burden of limitations – my own assumptions, rules, and agreements I made with myself to behave in certain ways. I'm releasing everything that makes me read life in this conditioned way. Life is not what it seems! It's definitely not limited to what scientists say! They can never measure the power of our minds or our hearts, can they? There's a big gap in our modern world, and it's all about the mystery of life itself. Being a human, and certainly being a medicine woman, is all about weaving together the material side of life – the body, desires, feelings, social connections, and what we do every day – with the unseen part of life, which very much dictates how we live it. One without the other is empty.

Exactly one year later, on Christmas Day, I sit with tobacco in a sacred way, praying and looking back on my last year. This time, Christmas is quiet – no extravagant adventures, just going within, allowing the long nights and darker days to orchestrate my life. I think of all the people I've met at the sound baths I facilitated, all the moments of deep connection, singing with my tribe, healing work, and going deeper in my relationship with nature.

I recall taking Changa and how I thought something brought me back to life, and I realize it was me. My own willpower brought me back. I smile to myself, knowing that I've just uncovered another source of power within me, a part of me so powerful and yet unknown to my awareness, from the shadow of unconsciousness. Life is a mystery indeed. There is always more to uncover, always more to learn.

I take time to give gratitude to everyone involved on my journey and to myself. This whole day and evening feels like a deep cleanse of the soil in my garden, making space for new growth next year.

It's Slow Progress

The first time I experienced non-locality was at a gong bath.

Perhaps that's why I'm so into sound healing.

I was in my twenties, confused and angry most of the time and not knowing why. I was self-medicating with alcohol, drugs, and sex. Movies and series stretched out to seasons on end also helped. I made myself busy with work, chores, and socializing. I was willing to do anything but spend time with myself. I didn't want to look any closer at the mess; deep down, I knew this would be a big job. Crushing mountains with a hammer kind of big. Who would want this? And what for? What was on the other side of all that inhuman effort?

One day, I was dragged to a gong bath by my friend and neighbor, Anya. She was telling me all about these sessions she'd been attending for a while now, how epic they were. I wasn't paying much attention, it sounded plain weird to me. But one day, she just took me with her, completely ignoring my resistance. How grateful I am to Anya that she rudely violated my desires to be left alone…

I arrive at the venue, just a simple space for hire in the city center in Łódź. People are already there, making themselves comfortable on yoga mats, with blankets and pillows. Anya smiles at me and finds her space in the front row, right next to the impressive collection of big, bad-ass looking gongs, maybe ten to fourteen of them, hanging neatly in two rows. I don't want to be so close. The facilitator looks weird and I can't wait for this whole thing to be over. I'm lying down, as comfortably as I can, the voice of the gong master streaming gentle guidance about resting, breathing, and letting the sounds in. And then, literally fifteen minutes later, the whole world shakes and shatters into a million pieces. And I am the epicenter of this explosion, the gongs vibrating through me. I completely forget that I have a body that's lying on the yoga mat. There's nothing of any locality there. People, buildings, gongs, cars outside – all this ceases to exist. There's just a great big vastness. You know what else ceases to exist? My petty little stories, desires, conflicting attitudes, things I thought were so important I could fight for them until the last blood. Other people's blood, that is, not mine. No, I was invincible in my ignorance and fierceness, in my personal, unresolved dramas. And they all just vanish. For the space of an hour, I am this non-local, non-material, all-encompassing, presence. Wow.

In the years that followed, I had a few more moments like this. After a 90-minute yoga session in South London in Savasana, when I let go of the heavy vinyasa practice. At ecstatic dance with Leigh in Bristol, when I let go of any ideas how to dance and let the body move itself, in abandonment. In sitting meditation practice, alone at home. Every time, it left me speechless. Excited. Confused. Because how do you even start to integrate this into your daily life? Everything in your life – compared to this – feels so flaky, unreal, empty. And there's this aversion to just carry on with life's chores. To go to work, empty the dishwasher, tidy the house. No thanks, I prefer to feel one with the universe again. There's even a reluctance to engage in social activities, to have relationships, because now they're distractions from the 'real truth'. Oh, what a mind-blowing puzzle that was. But the truth is, this experience of feeling boundless, limitless, one with all, invited me to stop seeing life as chores altogether. But it was so hard to see it then. Beyond my capacity to understand.

How we interpret a situation is tightly connected to where our mind is. Given my Christian upbringing, I could understand my experience as an encounter with God; if I was feeling anxious before or after the experience, I could call the space purgatory. There was nothing there. Just a great emptiness. No angels, no colors. Lots of feelings of uncertainty, so perhaps the design of this space was to await my judgment day? If I gave in to my fear, maybe I would even call it hell? A deadly space with no escape, no sense of individuality, no interactions with others… and if

I had a great day, felt at peace with myself, maybe I would call it heaven. Maybe I would feel completion, fulfillment. An all-encompassing presence. Only being. No doing. A non-local manifestation of Aya. Maybe I would say I met God the Almighty in His home?

Our feelings and our mindset dictate how we interpret our perception, every single moment. Most of the time, we're not even aware of it – we function on autopilot, right? Everybody knows that. But only a small percentage of people take it in. And a small percentage of those people allow it to move them, let it change how they act. This is not to say I'm one of them. On the contrary, I'm stubborn as fuck. I couldn't understand what happened, so I just stayed calm and carried on.

Heyoka

Let's roll, heyoka.

When my teacher introduced me to spirit animals, I was bewildered just how much wisdom the stories carry. The Native Americans tell these stories to their children and anyone who cares to listen. Every animal has its own date in the calendar. They all have a different teaching, providing metaphorical advice on how to deal with life's challenges in their own unique way. And they all belong. Flying, swimming, crawling, running, zigzagging – they all belong in the family of creatures.

The coyote has a very special place amongst them. A coyote is a trickster, a magician, a heyoka. Be careful when you come across one. He will surely make a fool of your old habits, he will laugh at your weakness, he will point out the parts of your persona that you try so hard to hide... indeed, heyokas are feared and respected. They bring pain, confusion, and suffering. They push your sensitive buttons. But their presence can be a blessing. When welcomed and embraced, they create an opportunity to reconnect with your core, with your deeper purpose, and will make you stronger. By means of their outrageous behavior, they simply ask a question:

"What are you doing? Do you really want this?"

When you meet a coyote with love and compassion, calmness and stillness, it becomes a dog, a loyal guardian and ally. It will guide you through paths that he knows and will protect you. But it takes courage to be still and focused on yourself rather than on the challenge.

On my journey to freedom, through a great struggle, I am becoming a Hollow Bone – a person with no buttons to push, no jealousy, no impulsive anger or chronic fear. It so happened that the coyote visited frequently and that after many encounters, we became companions. I am no longer petrified when it comes. I welcome the teachings. I bow my head in humbleness and ask for details.

My bullies, my early managers… they were all heyokas. So was Kirt. He came in disguise.

For one year, we were exchanging messages via WhatsApp. For one year, I slowly built up my love and trust for him. He always welcomed my wild, untamed nature. With his WhatsApp in my pocket, I was unfolding more and more into the old and new archetypes of the great goddess. I was taking him to my rituals, for my walks in nature in the middle of the night. I was exposing my sacred life to him; activities I rarely shared with anyone. A kind of behaviour that historically led to persecution; nearly 350 years of witch hunt. Kirt was there for me. Curious, kind, encouraging. He helped me to heal the shadow of the executions for witchcraft, proving that times have changed. The men are different. They are no longer afraid. They can be open and present, grounded. They can be strong in their power of stillness and light, and invite women to reconnect with the wildest storms to bring in more love, to bring in truth. And that's what we were doing. Until we met.

Set Your Oh-My-Gods Free

I'm sitting in LaMuella, Mandrem, North Goa. I've just finished my cardamom coffee and ordered a banana pancake. I feel high on the brew and gently absorb the atmosphere of this place. People are relaxed, talking quietly. A little self-awareness comes in, painfully, as I realize I was just the loudest person in this peaceful, nicely-designed mingling space.

I unexpectedly met a person I connected with six months ago at a ceremony in the UK. I mean, come on, what are the chances I would bump into her in this little café, in a quiet little Indian village by the Arabic sea? She said that the medicine man who facilitated the ceremony was here too. He was actually staying in a beach hut a ten-minute walk from mine, how about that? Of course, I was loud with my *oh-my-gods.* One thing led to another – Tara updated me on her life and told me she was considering moving to Bristol from London, and that I might be the right person to help her with this transition; that's why we met on the other side of the world! There are no coincidences, I'm telling you. It was a nice little reconnection. Then Tara went her way and I stayed on at LaMuella, allowing the excitement of the meeting to calm down.

Two blinks of an eye later, I meet the medicine man! I can't believe it… we exchange a long hug and a brief conversation, then I leave him be with his brunch, as I feel that this is what he wants. Wow. My heart is like a butterfly, flapping its wings softly, darting from one flower to another. I'm no longer sure if I'm high on the cardamom coffee or these connections. I can't believe this. LaMuella will always be a special place for me. This is where I met Kirt in Goa just over one month back. This is where the epic drama started with Dolina. This is the place where the first element of the domino fell silently down, starting the process of destruction, swallowing all my money, my heart, my identity. This is how I finally put all the pieces of the puzzle together.

Indah Desa – Beautiful Village

Kirt sends me a message. It's only a short one. He says that due to not being able to pay his bill in his current resort, he can't meet me at Indah Desa the following day. He has to focus all his time and effort on arranging the money. I look at the screen on my phone. This was going to be our first exclusive meeting. He and Dolina are now finished and renegotiating terms for their joint erotic business. I can only imagine just how fucked up life is for both of them right now. Suddenly you end up without your partner and no job… I'm trying not to feel guilty, but I'm only fifty percent successful. I know I'm not the reason for the mess between them – they've been working on it for a long time now, not letting each other in fully, not being brave or honest, not standing in their truth. But all this wouldn't have happened if not for me. Well, it wouldn't have happened then, and in the way it did.

I already paid for Kirt's last resort. It was just two weeks ago, on his last day at Mandala.

He stood in front of me, in his quirky celebrity style, a half-naked outfit. I could hear Dolina yelling at him through the phone. Her voice was loud that he moved the headset away from his ear. Still, he was taking it in. Finally, she hung up on him and he told me he fucked up.

Not the first time, I thought, but say nothing.

He explained to me in a sad, haunted tone that his American account was frozen. It was a Friday evening, his assistant was working on it but not well enough, the time difference… whatever. He didn't have money to pay his bill. I believed him. I offered to pay for it. He was reluctant.

"Of course I'm going to pay! Wouldn't you do the same for me? You will give me the money back when you have it, when all this mess clears up, don't worry! That's what friends do for each other, no?"

It came as a bit of a surprise that it was £1500.

Really? Wow. OK.

I already said I'd pay, there's no going back now.

That had been two weeks ago. They went off together to sort out their mess. He was messaging me every day, multiple times, complaining about how hard it was, missing me. He wanted to meet, and I agreed. Just for three days. Then he would go back to Dolina to continue building new structures after this nuclear disaster. They still had a lot of talking, a lot of mending to do. But he wanted a breath of fresh air, a recharge, a moment of creative fun that would perhaps give him the strength to go back to the drawing board, where every new architectural design falls before it's even expressed with a first line.

Okay. I was up for that. I was sooo up for that. He wanted a recharge and I knew exactly what I wanted. And I was so excited! Like Cinderella getting an invitation to the ball. I sang with the birds, ordered a new ball gown from my fairy godmother, and locked my ugly sisters and stepmother in the dungeon. I definitely didn't want the whole malarkey with a midnight run, losing the shoe… I was ready to receive him. Fully and completely. And now he was telling me his financial problems were still persisting.

Oh dear.

I'm sad that money has become a limitation for us. That it's preventing us from meeting alone for the first time. Uncensored. Unrestricted. Wild and free. So guess what I do. I offer to help him again. Two HiFix transactions and one sleepless night later, and we finally meet.

I feel so excited. I know we've met now to experience magic together. To venture beyond my limitations, to meet in a way I've never dared with anyone else before. I'm shaking a little. And to think we almost didn't meet at all… I shrug my hands, head, shoulders. Here he is now, right in front of me, and I see his quiet disconnection. I wonder for a moment if it's about money, his apocalyptic disaster with Dolina, or something else entirely. I give him time. I really just want to put our astronaut suits on and go, without telling Houston anything. I feel so ready and so impatient. So I give myself time too.

We have a long meal. Everything is delicious and I'm full. He orders two desserts from the menu. He's procrastinating. But I'm still working on giving him time, so I enjoy the chocolate brownie and fresh mango, heavenly suspended in deep layers of vanilla ice cream. I have very little space in my belly for this, so it's good to have time, yes. But it's getting late and I'm torn. I'm enjoying his company, the constant banter that comes through being present together and through self-abandonment. I love the freedom of self-expression, love the laughter and sexual tension I feel in both my heart and my pussy. I know what's coming later. With much resistance, finally, I let go of my feelings of impatience. The fight is over. Now there's just a lot of tickling for what's to come. And then, suddenly, the never-ending dinner is over and the vast horizon of the beach bar changes into the A-frame roof and four walls of the tiny beach hut. Most of the space here is taken by this enormous bed with white linen. It looks clean, cozy, and inviting. The walls are made of wood and palm leaves woven in tight patterns. I can hear every little noise happening outside these walls and realize I'll be heard there too. I feel a mix of shyness and excitement. He goes to the toilet, I check the bed. The toilet has a door, but he doesn't slide it closed for privacy. I smile. Now it's my turn to go. I pee in the shower. I look at my legs, being washed by clean water. I'm standing on a single tile made of stone, large enough for me to move around. Outside of my island, there's just beach sand and the water flowing right there. No soap. Just water, flowing naturally back into the earth. There's no roof over my head, just a safety net for coconuts, abundantly growing on every tree spiking high above my head, the grand seeds of the tall, fine, far-famed trees. The night is very warm. An abundance of insects have already started their opera – yes, what a grand musical backdrop for the ballet of two lovers to be. I notice the little light coming from the open door leading to the bedroom, a reminder and a welcome. I want this so much. I can't believe it's happening. I'm taking my time. No need to rush now. I look at the sky beyond the feather-like branches of the coconut trees, the little white silver lights of the stars in the black vastness between them. Yes, I'll be there tonight. I take it in with my breath; the thought, the view. The moment. The spaciousness between the stars. The spaciousness between an atom and its nucleus. An opening. What's possible and what's not? Tonight is the night for breaking the rules. I'm ready. I go back to the bedroom. He's lying on the bed, naked, fairy lights above his head. He looks like an angel. We look at each other and smile. There's a sensation of nervousness and joy as we are both in the unknown. We have an idea where we're heading, but the how… that's completely unscripted, unplanned, to be unfolded moment by moment in the emerging space between us.

Soon enough, everything unfolds all at once. My breath meets his breath, moved by waves of pleasure. My song comes out wild and untamed, changing tones and rhythm with our touch, with the movement of our hips. As I relax more and more into this dance, I breathe my violently building climax up into my heart and give it to him in a silent offering. He receives it. We are both right on the edge. It's not about having sex, it's not about coming. We're here to go beyond the climax, to glide on the energy of our feelings and sensations, rising up and reaching the Great Beyond. Beyond the senses, beyond logic and reason, even beyond dreams and desires. I'm here to experience a complete unison with another human being. I want to take him in completely and fully, on every level, allow him to enter the deepest folds of my existence.

I realize that this is exactly what's happening. The intention is being materialized by the body as every fiber of my being is aligned, in agreement with this. I now perceive his presence as a gigantic erection that I caress, lick, massage, with my hands, my voice, my breasts, my thighs. The totality of me wants to receive the totality of him, and I use my breath and my meditation to go deeper into this embodied, soulful experience. I inhale his sweat into my lungs – the sweet, warm scent of love, passion, and connection. I have a desire to give him everything that I am, all of it – the material, thoughts, feelings, energy... I put it all in my breath with an intention and give myself to him in complete surrender, exhaling directly into his mouth, his skin, hands, cock. I notice that the waves of movement are now supported by my whole body. His body. We gaze into each other's eyes. Stillness. Fire. Deep darkness of the pupils surrounded by light. Dangerous eyes. *Oh.* A very unexpected sting of fear. Strong, unnamed, primal.

I want this danger, this fear, this darkness, with no bottom, no floor.

I relax into my fear. I keep my gaze, calm. Now it's just stillness. His face is changing. Now he's got a set of three eyes on each side of his nose. He is a different creature, a being from another space, beyond time. I keep gazing, give myself permission not to try to understand, not to judge, allowing everything to be, and I keep relaxing, surrendering. Soon the eyes disappear, and where his face was is a deep black space with far-off flickering lights, like the night sky. I feel invited to go in. I lean over. Then I feel a strong pull on my arm and hear my name. His face is back, we're sitting on the bed, my pelvis on top of his, I'm moving gently on his cock. I kiss him. I want to go back. I relax into his gaze again and see the creature's eyes. Yes, I'm on a good track. Just keep relaxing, keep the gaze, past the fear and danger. The opening appears again. I'm so curious, I want to go. But he calls my name again and I'm back in the hut.

Okay.

Our wet bodies collapse on the bed and we share our

experiences.

"Wow."

"Yeah, wow."

I try to gather my thoughts.

Did that just happen?

I'm speechless, not sure where to start. I can't say how long we're in this silence. He is the first to speak. He tells me that at one point, he felt like I was sucking his whole being into my yoni.

"Your vagina became a cosmic spacetime with such a strong gravitational acceleration that nothing – no particles, no thoughts, not even light – could escape from it. I was resisting with all my might, hills in the concrete, and I was witnessing my willpower being gnarled and crushed in this pull. I didn't know what would happen if you didn't stop."

I bite my lips with an improvised, innocent smile.

Yes, I remember moving not only my pelvis but my whole body in changing directions, from spirals to forward-backward, to up and down, to stillness, to spirals again. My ankles, knees, and thighs moving on his pelvis, my hands reaching and gathering his energy from the head, throat, hands, and feet to the center, from behind him and through him, focusing it into his cock and allowing it into my yoni. Yes, I wanted all of him in.

He tells me about an erotic scene in *American Gods* he saw recently, where this black goddess sucks her victim in, taking his energy and leaving him dry and dead. He was certain that this is what was going to happen to him if we continued any longer.

I look at him with a silent question, but he doesn't say anything else. I'm not sure what to make of this. I just experienced a total act of surrender, giving this man everything I was, and I motioned openness, a current to receive nothing less.

I stay with my mixed feelings for a while. What he said confused me. He was dead serious. He didn't tell me to stop then. But he did stop me later. I tell him about my experience with his face and he recognizes it instantly.

"Yes, yes, I had to call you back, I felt you going and I wasn't sure if we would find our way back if I let you in. I didn't want to lose you. I had to call you back."

I close my eyes and allow my mind and body to drift away in the natural resting space of sleep. Slowly, my feelings fade – the excitement for having discovered new lands, disappointment for not putting my feet there, and surprise to see him afraid and unwilling to go. He's been talking about it so much. Oh, well – maybe another time.

We spend two more days together, eating, swimming, sun drying on the beach, giggling, sharing stories. The nights are passionate, but not tantric. On the third morning, he packs his stuff in his little bag and leaves. A simple act of leaving. Before he walks away, he looks at me and catches my mood, the dry tears in the corners of my lips and the silent scream in the forced stillness of my eyes. He tells me:

"I could stay, we could rent a flat together, move in, enjoy each other's company, get a dog. You want a child, I decide to give it to you; one or two, then I lose interest in you and the family, you are constantly exhausted, we argue so much, we start to look for happiness outside of us, and the whole cycle starts again."

He plants a kiss on my bewildered cheek and walks away, his rubber flip-flops kicking the sand up behind him. I look at the empty space he left in me.

A dog? Children?

Not the first time, I am being misunderstood. Not the first time, I am hearing a sad, painful opinion made by a man who thinks he knows what my problem is and what my solution should be. It used to fuel my anger to a breaking point of collision. To be unseen, unheard, misjudged. To be completely disregarded as an individual with a unique story, in favor of their own judgmental stereotype of a woman. Feeling belittled, not important. And most times, I'd put up a fight with tears and blood, challenging their viewpoint, forcing them to see Me. And on those occasions when my battle was successful, making space for my voice, I'd forget what the message was in the first place. End result of collision: "Women don't know what they want." Despair. Hopelessness. And a sea of pain. That's how it used to be. Now I own my stories, and I don't take other people's stories personally. When I experience a man exercising his power by telling me what's what, I take it as it is – his opinion. He's telling me a story about himself and how he reads the situation. A different perspective. The child, the flat, losing interest and all that – those are all his fears. He also revealed just how far he is from the freedom I'm seeking.

I stay at Indah Desa for a few more days, giving myself time to reflect and integrate this experience. The staff here is very nice. I make friends with a woman who comes to clean my hut. One time, she points at the Shiva amulet I got from Kirt, a little brass figurine of a god, dancing in a mandala. It hangs casually on the wall, between my dresses. With a mix of gesturing, a little English vocabulary, and lots of smiling, she explains that she prays to this god every day. I ask her to tell me her favorite story of Shiva. I know this god through my yoga practice: Shiva the creator, protector and god of wisdom. Also Shiva the master of thieves, villains, and beggars. I love hearing old stories and receiving the gift of wisdom and blessing through them. So I beg her, even though I see that she's very shy, hiding her smile in her hand. When she finally decides to do it, she just gives me a one-sentence kind of story.

"Shiva destroys the universe and then the new Creation begins."

When I get her story, my body goes into spasms. I feel

extremely cold and shiver uncontrollably in the forty-degree heat. I give her thanks, bow my head to her, and offer her the amulet. She tells me she can't receive it. I tell her I would like her to pray with it, begging her to take it, and eventually, she does.

Part Three

"You do not have to walk on your knees
for a hundred miles through the desert repenting.
You only have to let the soft animal of your body love
what it loves."

Mary Oliver

Astronaut's End

I met Kirt two more times. The last time was in Sukhumvit, one of the most exclusive and expensive areas in Bangkok. We stayed two nights in a skyscraper hotel, with a see-through en-suite and a window view so far and high that I felt I was in heaven. There was a rooftop swimming pool and bar, accessible only to the wealthiest visitors in BKK. This world was new to me. Traveling on a budget, I would never consider a place like that – yet here I was, feeling at home, comfortable with all this wealth around me, not intimidated or belittled by it, smiling to everyone around me and listening to Kirt's plan to open a Tantra Temple.

"Aya, you are so special, so alive, so sexual. You are a natural tantra goddess. You will be the living Goddess in the temple. People will desire you so much, you will see them fucking you with their eyes. You will constantly feel aroused in this beehive of sexual desire. How would you feel about making love to me publicly, connecting like we did in India? I think this would be a big part of it; letting people witness that kind of connection, it will allow them to access it themselves, by proximity. We will climb the highs together, and people will join… and of course, there will be some instructions, we all need to be on a level here, but the goal is to experience it, not learning by listening, if you know what I mean."

He was conveying his vision to me; a picturesque, grand design for people to awaken through sexuality. He was telling me about his wealthy entrepreneurial contacts, about the building plans, and kept reminding me how special our experience was, how unique I was.

I listened to him attentively, but didn't want to look at him. From my soft velour chair in the rooftop restaurant, I observed the sun enclosing its arch and getting ready to kiss the horizon. I had heard all this before, via WhatsApp, in his everyday messages to me when we were away. I had many questions, but I didn't voice them. The prevailing longing was to stand on the edge of that abyss again and kiss the world I knew goodbye. That's what I wanted.

He asked me what I was thinking.

If you need to build a temple to make the jump, you might as well go ahead and do that.

But here were the bare bones of the truth. The reason why we didn't make the jump together was because of his fear and lack of trust. We only came to the edge of the abyss once, that first night at Indah Desa. He never made it past his fear. He didn't have the clarity of intention. He didn't trust my wisdom. There were still matters he hadn't dealt with now, deeply hidden and unavailable, making alignment impossible. Now he was investing all his time in this grand design for a temple to keep himself occupied, because if he stopped for a moment and looked within, he would know he really ought to deal with the fear and lack of trust first.

I know, it's easy for me to say, I've done the work. But I haven't forgotten just how painful these appointments were, and how much courage and endurance they require. So I said nothing. I looked at him. He was explaining about other Tantric Ashrams he knew and had been to, telling me why they weren't genuine and where they failed. I could see that he preferred our relationship to be one of master and disciple. He loved giving me lectures and quoting gurus, both new and old. He was indeed very intelligent and had an extremely good memory. He was also gifted with his language and his use of words. He almost convinced me that the wisdom he shared with me is his truth. But it wasn't, it came from the books he read. It's wasn't lived. Now I saw the truth. The idea of the temple was to domesticate me – give me purpose, keep me busy while he could procrastinate, cashing money from this spiritual business and getting intoxicated with power from being so close to the source. He was promising me the heaven of being desired by the masses, where I could sing, drum, gong, whatever I wanted. Just a pretty reeve of enticing sentences, hanging on a closed door. When I spoke of what I wanted, he didn't like it that much. But he was intelligent enough not to say no to me. He was a master weaver and was using all his skills to create a perfect illusion for me.

But I am Black Lilith. My wisdom is not from books. I came to this point the slow and sweaty way, through working with my shadow. My wisdom is embodied. So is my life. So is my truth. I live it and I die it.

The sun went over the line of the horizon and started its journey on the other side of the green-blue planet. There were no stars to be seen from the rooftop of my exclusive hotel – only the lights of the city and pollution. Tired, I told him I'd had enough for today. For a while, we just gazed into each other's eyes. I wanted to believe he could do it; that he could go past his fear and that maybe one day, he would trust me. We went to our room and I let him fuck me. He did it doggy-style, rough, on the dark, thick carpet, me bent over the leather bench and looking through the full-size window, watching the faraway movement of the night lights of the city. City of Angels. That's how it translates, apparently. That's what he told me today. No. It actually translates as Village of Wild Plums. One ripe, one green…

My Basket is Empty. What Happened to my Apples?

I wake up in my boutique hostel in Bangkok. Boutique is a fancy name for a place that's not quite a backpacker lodging and not quite a hotel. It's a quirky design put together by someone with a bit of a budget and fair taste in architecture. My bed is big and comfortable, and the en-suite consists of a shower over the toilet enveloped closely by black, shiny tiles reflecting just a glimmer of light. There's no wardrobe, just industrial-looking hangers on the wall. A zigzag of LED lights is built into the edges of the dropped ceiling. The walls are white and gray with an occasional photo here and there. Not bad. It's just that the smell of sewage is making me resistant to breathe, and long brown stains on the walls are telling me stories of the monsoon last season, maybe the season before too?

I'm flabbergasted. These otherwise dry and indifferent walls have been deeply penetrated by the tears from the sky falling with so much persistence they broke the seals of the roof. Yes, I know how it feels. My pain is breaking the seals of my identity; a bottomless well of darkness with no way out. I'm completely immersed in the experience of despair, loneliness, grief, and lost hope. My tears join the stains on the walls. My loud cries are filling this sad place, saturating it with the vibrations of the dark night of the soul. It's a good fit.

Kirt told me not to ask him for anything. Of course, I asked him for my money. I gave him all my money and was living on the little bit left on my credit card. He confidently delivered an elaborate tale making me believe that he was a magician when it comes to money; he can materialize it, but he needs to be worry-free. The minute he contracts in anxiety, his ability to make money becomes very limited. It made sense to me. You lose your freedom of thought and creativity and you lose the ability to make money. Fine, okay. I'll keep my financial status to myself. I think he knows I literally gave him all my money. I think he remembers my words when I gave him the last bit of it.

I visited Kochi at the time of their annual international art biennale. It's the biggest art festival in Asia – a complete immersion in the dream weave of modern creators, musicians, performers, artists of all kinds. A sensual feast for my eyes, ears, sense of poetry, and beauty. A magnificent mirror communicating my soul back to me in the form of paintings, sculptures, performances, and happenings. It took me two weeks to experience the full extent of it. Two weeks of art, beautiful Indian food, new connections with creators from all around the world, and lots of random adventures.

It didn't really matter to me that I was on a bowl of rice – since I gave all my money away and was patiently waiting for it to make its way back to me, I was on a very tight budget. No taxis or tuk-tuks, no fancy restaurants, just a bowl of rice once a day, no alcohol, no treats, just walking and digesting the art world. A very humbling experience. Simple. And yet so rich.

Every day I received exciting messages from Kirt, as usual with lots of banter, of course, and updates about the temple he was designing, stories of how he was missing me, loving me, wanting to further explore the universe beyond the limits of his mind, through the gateway of our unison, and about his slow progress with Dolina. A time came when he asked me for more money.

"Oh my God, Aya, this is so annoying. I'm so close and so far away at the same time. I want to meet you, I have to meet you soon. I want to just be with you and create the temple together. To do all that, I am building a bridge and it's almost done. I'm building from one shore and the opposite at the same time, and all I need is a final piece, just one bolt, to put those two together, seal them, have the bridge standing. It's so silly. Such a tiny little thing standing in the way to be with you, to make the dream come true."

"What is that thing, Kirt?"

"£1000. It's nothing compared to what I've already manifested. But it makes our meeting impossible."

"I gave you so much already. I can give it to you, but this is all I've got. I have nothing left."

I bet you're in disbelief and maybe even getting a little annoyed with me. You're probably asking yourself what I could possibly be thinking? My 17-year-old niece would have advised me not to do this. My mum, if she'd lived, would feel my longing and whisper: *This is not the way.* My friends, if I'd told them, would have shouted:

"No, Aya!"

But I didn't listen. I think that was the reason I didn't share my adventure with anybody. I knew how ridiculous it would sound to anyone outside of the equation.

I was thinking about that commitment I made at Indah Desa, when I was deeply immersed in tantric union with him. A commitment to give him everything, including my last breath. I literally had nothing left. I stripped myself from my friends, the sense of purpose in my life, the moral compass that used to guide my recognition of right and wrong, good and evil. I had no more dignity or self-respect. All I had was the last bit of money that would allow me to buy a ticket back home.

It made perfect sense; I was being tested on my word. I couldn't just declare I was ready to give everything up, and when the time came – when I had to take the risk – simply back off. Nope. I had to be all in. I really wanted to go into that abyss. This was just another form of fear, I thought – a very real fear of being hungry and stranded homeless in a faraway country – but a fear nonetheless. I had to be loyal to myself. So.

Here it is. I'm fully in. Whatever it takes. With this last bit of money, I let go of hopes and desires for the future. The courage to do so isn't coming from my mind. My mind is throwing curses at me for being foolish. So I take time to negotiate with myself.

We have to try. We've explored and exhausted all other avenues in the past. This is a once in a lifetime opportunity to bungee-jump into freedom from the monetary rules of this world. Freedom from the illusion of safety that having money creates. If we don't try now, we might be closing a door on something of great importance.

This is a tantric moment I'm having with myself. It's a heart connection based on complete surrender. I make the choice to let go of the idea that I need money, and I immediately experience a great expansion of energy – a powerful surge of adrenaline created by my body with just a thought. A choice I just made. The new chemical composition in my brain makes my body tingle. I surrender to this feeling, allow myself to be in this aliveness of blood rushing through my veins, my heart beating fast. In other circumstances, I might have read this state of the body as an acute anxiety attack. But because I made my choice open-heartedly, there is no fear. It feels like my body and the space around me is being reverberated to a different frequency. For most of the day, I am spaced out.

I send him money and the next day, he gives me the date and place for our next meeting.

How exciting! Finally, we're getting to work!

A couple of days later, I arrive in Bangkok, at the hotel he chose, and am again surrounded by wealth in the form of marble and gold. The room he rented has so many light switches it takes him a solid thirty minutes to check them all until he finds just the perfect combination of light and shade. Then he takes me to dinner. He says he thinks he knows just the place for me. To my surprise, it's a tacky restaurant with fake oversized flowers, a pond with a plastic buddha, and too many tables, making it impossible to navigate between them.

Is this what he thinks of me? Plastic flowers and buddha?

The music annoys me, the menu annoys me, the moisture on my skin is being annoyingly sucked by the plastic chair I sit on. I decide to go to the toilet for a breather, only to find it dirty and smelly. I use the anger and disappointment to reignite my intention. Yes. I want this. I am happy to see him. More so, I'm excited about going beyond the known land of the conscious mind. I can't wait. I would have skipped dinner – my stomach is tiny now anyway. But I'm here. I'm trying to be gentle with him. He dominates the evening with stories about Dolina. She's such a big part of his life. Being present is a little hard, and I realize I had a lot of expectations for this meeting, all of them slowly dissolving in the dust between his stories.

Bit by bit, his words crush them to pieces, and the spaces between blow the little particles of what's left from my desires into the air. Puff. Gone. Sadness.

It's okay, just let it be. Life is never what I imagine it to be anyway. Just keep surrendering. Yes, let the melody of his voice be the anchor for the present moment. Breathe.

But his stories are not of the now. He is as much in the past and future as anyone else in this plastic garden. The food comes and it's disappointing, but it serves as a tool to be here and now.

Just taste the miso soup. Feel your bum on the chair. Take it all in. Take all the feelings and thoughts in. Stay present with all of it.

Unexpectedly, a few gentle tears form in my eyes, and I'm moved by the feeling of complete and utter compassion for myself, for him, for the people that put the plastic buddha in the middle of the pond. He pays the bill and we head back to the luxurious white Egyptian cotton.

After this challenging start, we have two wholesome days and nights being fully present with each other. Sex takes us to places we've never been before; I get to express a violent and masculine side of myself that I never knew existed. I get to experience a chain of orgasms so long, I give up and die, accessing realms of a different nature, and eventually to come back to this realm in a new energetic configuration. I pleasure him in ways that bring him new insights and breakthroughs. I cover him and everything around him in my menstrual blood, releasing the ancient wild creatures within me, invoking power with symbols I never knew of until the wisdom comes instinctively, in the moment.

All of this happens in complete openness, trust, and surrender to each other. He drinks from my well and I use his fire to reconnect to the ancient wisdom within me. No limits. No looking back. It feels to me that we're warming up for the grand finale. That we're building momentum, a map for venturing into the portal again.

It must have been a late evening of the second day. My perception of time was distorted, because I was fully engaged in the unfolding of events that didn't comply with the expected routines of day and night. My eyes were closed, my head enveloped in the softness of the pillow, in the spaciousness of deep restful breaths.

Just before falling asleep, I'm asked what I would like to happen next. I feel completely satisfied and exhausted. I don't know what I want next. In a slow, quiet voice, I finally find the words to say:

I feel that we are in a very vulnerable moment in time; we are weaving a thread together, made of a white cloud fluff. So fragile. It requires us to tend this weaving with great care. One moment, when we both feel ready, it will be possible to create magic together with this thread, and yes, invite others to join. I just want to close my eyes and rest now. I am happy you are here. Parting with you would be so violent, I can't even imagine. Let's just rest.

The next morning, he talks a lot about everything and anything. We don't make love. I take a shower, then he does. And then he says he needs to leave in thirty minutes.

"I need to get a taxi to get my stuff from the storage in my previous hotel, otherwise they will charge me extra."

It becomes clear to me that he is leaving. He talks some more about arranging our next meeting, but I put my finger on his mouth and shush him. I don't want to plan our next meeting, I want to be here and now. Here and now is very violent, annihilating everything we've been building. I look in his eyes and whisper through my clenched throat:

"I want to feel this moment," and he stops talking.

We sit for a while, the oblivion spreading to every corner of this room. It's all gone. We get packing and take the elevator downstairs. The receptionist has all the dirty towels in a clear bag, talking loudly, making a case to charge extra for laundry. I catch her angry gaze. She is condemning me. She thinks I should be ashamed. I remember making every towel dirty. I smile at her, thinking:

If you only knew…

I watch Kirt paying extra and we sit on the fancy sofas, waiting for his taxi. Bad traffic, apparently – the driver is late. I take his hand. The tears in my throat aren't coming out.

Are they going in?

I'm balancing on the edge of a knife. I find a way to vocalize the chaos in my head and heart.

"I'm so grateful to you for all the gifts you bring into my life. But this is really sad for me. I thought we met to start creating together. I thought this was it. The final bolt in the bridge was there. And now you are saying goodbye to me. There is nothing beyond this point. Everything is blurry. I feel I am standing on the edge of an abyss. Let me be here. I'm actually really grateful to you for everything that happened. This is what I feel now. Gratitude. I got to experience so much magic with you. I let myself go so wild – fully myself, with no inhibitions. It's been a privilege and a bliss. I feel both – love and joy and utter sadness and despair. I've actually never felt more pain than this, now. I don't know how it is possible.'

I cry. A few tears escape my eyes and nose. He speaks his gratitude and then he leaves. I look at his taxi for a moment, take my rucksack, and venture outside looking for a café where I can hide for a moment. When it's overflowing, it's better to let it out. So I cry. I cry so heavily, the tears cover every landmark in the creation of Aya. It rains so bad, the tears turn into an ocean; the great flood. There is nothing left standing. No dry land. Just the vast stretch of deep water. Time is passing. I cry some more, looking at

Booking.com, trying to find a place to sleep tonight, unable to plan anything beyond this. Let's just survive today. I find a bunk bed with breakfast for £3.00. Perfect. I cry all through my taxi journey, then at the reception when I check in.

"Are you okay, madam?"

"Yes, sorry, I'm okay."

She shows me my little bed and I settle my tears there in a spiral motion, going outward and inward at the same time. My knees tucked into my arms, I fall asleep. The next morning, I check my wallet, my bank accounts, and realize just how bad my finances are. I send Kirt a message – I need his help to get food and accommodation. And that's how I land in my shitty situation, with stained walls and ceiling.

I wanted this. I wanted all of this. Nobody forced me. I know somehow this is happening perfectly for me, I just can't see it clearly, can't understand, because I am in this ocean of tears and snot. Maybe I could see the bigger picture if I could only generate some curiosity about this, just for a moment. What would the bigger picture be?

I'm with this question for half a day now, in my tacky tired place of forgotten fashion, until I just can't anymore. I put some clothes on and go for a walk. Hungry. Lost. Confused.

How deep is pain?

And what are your limits? Pain is as deep as you dare to go. The same with love, fear, joy… I was so open. Giving love, compassion, everything I am and everything I had. The payment was the death of ego. Maybe at some point in the future, someone will read this novel by chance and think:

Really? Is that how people used to go through transformation and awakening? How barbaric!

They wouldn't believe it. All this expansion of pain will be long gone. But this is where we are now. Look at the world around us. Pain and suffering come from every direction. It comes from within as well. This is where I am. I want to keep going. Full commitment. I believed that this magic with Kirt was going to take me to full awakening, and I also believed that with every crisis, I was shedding a skin; another layer of limitations created entirely by my own mind. I wanted to be absolutely free. I wanted to be the embodiment of unconditional love, in every circumstance, for everyone, everywhere. I was willing to die for it. And believe me, it physically felt like dying. The fear of dying was real. The pain of dying was real. And I did find love. More than I could handle. But what happened to my freedom? I didn't want Kirt to choose my hotels. I wanted to choose them and pay for them myself. I needed money for food too. I needed to budget for myself. I told him I didn't want to depend on him for accommodation and meeting my basic needs. He agreed and said he would give me some money soon. It felt like I was still in the vastness of the great flood with no sight of dry land. I forbid myself to dwell on it too much. I needed time.

This is all going to be okay in the end.

I find a bunk bed in a friendly-looking hostel. Four beds in my room, breakfast and coffee included. Okay. I check in and immediately connect with the girl on the bed next to mine. She's from Japan, an outsourced PA for an estate agency in the US who works as a satellite, independently from the geographic base of the office. So she takes her laptop to various places in the world. She travels a lot. Perhaps our connection is so strong because she too can see the world from the flip side. Her working hours are aligned to whatever is daytime in America. She often works at night, alone, to the sounds of dream time around her. She is so soft and gentle. I like her sad, lonely smile. I think I recognize my smile in her. I don't want to share my story with her, so I just keep asking her questions, and she allows a free flow of stories about her job, places she traveled to, her relationship with a man in Canada. The bunk beds are made of metal and are a bit bigger than usual, the AC is on, and I'm naked under my duvet. I'm gently falling asleep and she's getting ready for work. Her life seems so different and so familiar. We are two passersby heading in different directions – two trains heading to opposite destinations but standing at adjacent platforms. Just for a moment, we connect. No obligations, no assumptions, no expectations. Finally, she asks me about my story. I tell her in my sleepy, slow voice that I'm on a quest for ultimate freedom and unconditional love. And in her silence, I feel that she gets me. There is no judgment, no advice, no comment. Just a silent recognition. When she comes out of stillness, she finishes packing her stuff and leaves the room. I close my eyes and fall asleep.

Kirt told me that the moment he wakes up in the morning, he creates the whole universe. Everything. Including me. And for some reason, he always creates the same thing; a continuity of yesterday.

I know I exist independently from him, even when he is asleep. I don't tell him that. What's the point? He would say I'm supposed to say this, to question his enlightenment. He also says there's nothing outside of this moment. There was no yesterday, there was no date of birth, there was no morning. All those stories are created right now, in this moment, by his mind. Of course, at various times, I questioned him, challenged his opinions. He has an answer to everything. Sometimes his stories add up, equally as often they contradict themselves. It's fascinating though. I love listening to his explanations, even if they're way beyond my embodied experience and wisdom. These conversations are just pauses anyway. Entertaining distractions. What I'm really interested in is going beyond any thoughts, any opinions, into the land of oneness with all, the place where we came from. And he is here to help me. He is here to show me every obstacle, every single limitation I have in the form of assumptions, old programming, values… I'm fully committed to doing whatever it takes. I'm like a dog fully engrossed in watching a tasty piece of steak on the table. My complete attention is on it. I know I can't have it in this instant, but it's within my reach and I'm not giving up on it. Not for a tennis ball, not for a walk. But here's the thing. Kirt is avoiding me. He's keeping me at a distance, doesn't want to meet. Our only contact is via WhatsApp.

I've done everything.

He is scared. He knows I'll steer our meeting to try again, and he is not ready.

So what else can I do?

Here's one thing I haven't done: I haven't tried to let go of him.

It feels contradictory and very final.

What if I succeed?

Closing the door on Kirt might actually close my opportunity here. But I've tried everything else…

I spend a couple of days with this idea. Still on a tight budget, I don't want to wait a lifetime for him to get ready. Slowly but surely, I grow fond of my idea. My path so far demanded that I risk everything and subsequently lose everything; old friends, my career, my motherland, money, most of my identity, my boyfriend. It's time to risk losing him too. I'm going to do it. So I send him the most dramatic voice message in which I state explicitly, clearly, and in detail, leaving no room for confusion or doubt, that I'm letting him go. His response is immediate. He doesn't want that. He knows for a fact that if we close that door, it would be over-over. And that he would not make it, because I'm his heart. That's what he says. I'm all the love in his life.

How can I go away if I'm his heart? How can I leave this man to die?

But I must. I tried everything else and it didn't take me any closer to what I want; for this man to surrender completely, and for us both to go beyond.

And who knows what feasts are awaiting there…

We speak on the phone for over an hour, going back and forth with this breakup, and I realize that we've become a relationship.

Where did that creep in?

But it did. And it melted all the tantra like a fresh, hot piece of toast melts butter. We are now saturated with expectations. I want him to do this and that. Suddenly there are rules I need to follow and compromises that need to be made. Not because we want to, but because we must. We are now in a relationship, it's expected, I'm a girlfriend now, and that means something. In my case, it means my spontaneity is banned. I shall now focus only on his needs and put mine aside, for later or for never.

Wow. My freedom is gone further away than I thought. I've become a slave to my own set ideas.

This is creating a lot of inner conflicts and tension that's reflected in my communication with him.

Okay then.

I leave the tug-of-war for a moment and go for a walk. It's late in the evening. I find a little Ganesha shrine on the street, outside somebody's home. Just a statue with lots of flowers and food offerings – apples and curry in plastic bowls. I sit in front of it. This is perfect. Ganesha is an outside-of-the-box thinker. HIs actions, always unexpected and very clever, always get him where he wants to be.

One time, Shiva, his father, asked his three sons gathered around him to race around the world. The first one to complete the task would be granted a great reward. The two older and much stronger brothers left immediately, confident they would win. Ganesha stood there a moment, deep in thought. With a smile, he encircled Shiva, who is the whole world, and he got the reward.

I need this quality in me right now. I need to let go of the romantic relationship with Kirt, I need to free myself up from the role of girlfriend. To be free. To be love.

Call me crazy, but I know I'm capable of changing my life in a split second. So are you. The only thing that's required is the decision. Not just a statement. Every fiber of your being needs to be in agreement and ready to commit fully. That's all it takes. This one isn't so difficult at all. I'm already willing to do this when I send my message to him.

Gosh, I can be so dramatic, that message was really something.

I sit in front of Ganesha, chicken in my hands as an offering. This chicken came from the noodle soup I bought earlier. I'm an aspiring vegan, but I always fail to communicate it to the street food chefs, so I end up feeding cats and dogs with it. Today it goes to Ganesha. I have tears in my eyes and my skin is prickly with goosebumps when I make my statement to the empty darkness of the night.

"I want to be girlfriend-free in this relationship. And all future relationships with men for that matter. My deepest desire is to be completely and ultimately free."

I hear myself speak these words and feel them on every level.

"Free to engage in the totality of life with no expectations. Free to perceive the nature of everything as it is. Free to feel love as the natural fabric of this creation in a blazing hot way."

I pay for my prayer with chicken and sit for a moment in silence, in the warm soup of the air in old central Bangkok. That's it. It's done. I find my way back to my bed. I feel deeply moved.

I have weird dreams at night, and in the morning, I realize that I can't free myself from the trap by declaring it once. The blueprint of 'girlfriend' is there, hanging, ready to be embodied again. I have a feeling it will creep in once more, silently, unnoticeably.

The next few days I spend meditating in Buddhist temples, walking the polluted roads of Bangkok, reflecting, trying to reach the inner silence again and again. It's just me and myself. No money to go somewhere, do something exciting. It really is only me.

I go very deep in my sitting, walking, living meditation. I realize that Kirt has become my whole world now. He's a one-person representation for everything – all my lovers, friends, acquaintances, the wisdom in the world, weathers, the whole of the creation – in one half-naked, sex-oriented guru body. I realize that quitting my romantic relationship with him automatically ended my romantic attitude to the world. It had a profound effect on me. I went to the extreme opposite of loving it – complete detachment. The feelings had no effect on me anymore. I was simply neutral about everything that happened – as neutral as the mountain overhanging a river. Completely indifferent. All the drama that happened with Kirt, all the beauty I was seeing in the temples where I meditated, the funny people I encountered – they didn't move me. Only when this extreme opposite eased off a bit did I feel the terror of how it was. A world of no feelings. I didn't like it much.

Can I bring those two worlds together? Somehow find the slim little line where complete freedom meets the idea of being in a loving relationship with myself, nature, and humans?

I don't communicate with anyone. I continue being with myself the whole time. I sit on a beanbag in a warehouse-design hip hostel. I've been in deep meditation for most of last week, in the heat of this tropical climate, on a bowl of rice a day. Deprived of basic cultural and social comforts. Everything taken away from me. Dark clouds of doubt crowd my mind. I don't know who I am anymore, I don't know what reality is anymore. I feel the pressure building around me. It pushes me from every direction. It's difficult to breathe, like there's no air – just darkness. This familiar darkness beyond time, space, and creation. There's something in me that's not letting me move. I feel depleted of my resources. I feel my rivers have been dried, dammed, violated with toxins. Foreign waste in my oceans, in the air, on the ground. My depths in the ground are drilled, made hollow, robbed of all crystals, minerals, and the black blood of oil. I'm still breathing. Giving. Loving. I would like to stop someone. Hold them accountable.

How did it get to this state? Can't you see you are hurting me? But who is responsible? Is anybody listening?

The pain is overwhelming. I realize that I've tapped into the archetypal pain of the Earth. Soon, the story disappears and all that's left is pain. It stretches into all directions. There are no limits to it. It's infinite. It fills the whole space inside and out. There's nothing else, no one witnessing it – no body. Pain is all there is. A crushing dark force. I become the all-filling, limitless presence with no boundaries again. Everything is one. But this time, the one is pain. I lose the perception of time.

Did I pass out?

I'm back in my body, and I feel I'm suffocating.

Am I dying?

That night, I lucid dream in between being awake. I'm no longer certain what's a dream and what's real, but as stubborn as I am, I keep agreeing to my experience, keep inviting it, keep surrendering to it.

It feels like an eternity before the first light of sunrise finally makes its way through the little window. My eyes are half-closed, my face feels swollen, and my body is trembling.

What the fuck is happening to me? Am I going to survive this? Is this really what I want?

Fear. I'm afraid I'm mad. I'm afraid that people will come and lock me in a mental institution. Now that would be funny. I imagine myself ambitiously pushing toward freedom, locked in a hospital against my will, but for the safety of my life.

Something in me is broken. I'm exhausted and completely spaced out. I really just want a day of pleasure and rest. I pack my bikini, fill my empty plastic bottle with filtered water available for free at the reception, and walk thirty minutes to a hotel with a swimming pool on the roof. Confidence is the key. Yes. I put my feet on the clean shiny tiles, sending a message that I belong here. Not too fast, not hesitant. I walk past the reception. I find the elevator and press the button. I'm in. I go all the way up and a moment later, I'm enjoying the bubbles in the jacuzzi, tickling my bum and back. No money in my pocket but all the freedom in the world. The freedom to choose, to act. And a much wider vision of what's available to me. From this rooftop, I can see what real freedom is. I feel very happy and sad at the same time. It feels whole. Happiness without sadness is just one side of the polarity. Happy and sad at the same time encompasses it all. Actually, as I come to think of it, I create duality the moment I try to explain my feelings to myself, and in doing so, I limit my experience.

Okay. Let's just be some more in this state of no thoughts.

That's where I experience the all-fulfilling presence, the totality of everything in a completely satisfying way.

Yes. This is it. This is what I've been hunting for all this time.

This is what I thought I needed Kirt for. Plus, I just love drama. Kirt, being an outstanding drama queen himself, was a valuable co-creator of this mess. All that time, all I needed to do was stop and relax fully into my experience – whatever it is – in its totality, and I can access it instantly. But this stopping and relaxing fully is so difficult and so unavailable to my stubborn personality that I need an emotional tsunami to stop me. I need the collective shadow of our dying home planet to force me. I need multiple orgasms with a guy who's a mix of a celebrity, guru, and porn star. I need complete poverty in a faraway exotic country with no friends.

Isn't it paradoxical?

And funny. You've got to enjoy a joke when you get it, even if the joke is on you.

I decide not to think about the consequences of this insight. I just let myself be here, on this rooftop, feeling at peace with the complexity of my mind. Everything makes perfect sense to me now, including last night. I get it. The last line of resistance is defeated. Whatever is to come next, I'm ready. Not with patience, nor courage or strength. Not even with hopes to grow or go beyond anything or anywhere. Just with openness and presence.

The solution to Kirt comes the following morning, with his thirty-six-minute voice message. He asks me for more money. He advises me to really focus on this, make an effort, push through my limitations, this is really important for him and the tantra temple. This is exactly the message I need to end this adventure. I press record on my WhatsApp without the loving feeling of a devoted disciple. I press it with the love of an oak tree growing strong atop a hill.

Kirt, I gave you everything. You've been drinking from my well freely and with no limits. Many times I heard you crying, moved by my kindness, trust, and love. And then, when I thought I had no more to give, that my well was dry, I went down with a bowl and collected every single drop remaining from the cracks between the rocks. And when you asked for more, I went and I drilled other wells, sweat and pain, and I gave to you from there. And every time I poured water on you, it was like gashing it in the sand. Puff. Gone. Nothing grew out of it. We are not creating anything. We are not even together. You are traveling with your ex, and honestly, I don't know what it is that you do. We've spent six days together in the last ninety days. This is going nowhere. Kirt, I gave you almost £4000. The last chunk of money was my ticket back home. You said you were going to give it back to me. It's time that you pay it back. I will never give you any money ever again. It feels so good to say no to you.

It feels so right. Every molecule of my body is dancing, cheering for me.

How amazing to have told him how I feel. Yes. I was never that clear with him before. Now he will see me.

But he doesn't. He says I'm unenlightened, that I cling to my money. I'm bad energy and he doesn't want to see me again. He also says he will never give me my money back.

It should hurt me. But it doesn't. Instead, I felt a gushing wind of freedom. Obviously he is not a guru. Obviously all his 'wisdom' is stuff he reads in his books, iced like a cake with a sweet layer of charisma and sprinkled with a celebrity-style persona. My rose-tinted glasses are gone and I see him for who he truly is: an outstandingly clever con-man with above-average intelligence, a spiritual passerby who somehow gained insight into cosmic dimensions without sorting his shit out first. I fell for his light – I thought it was his and I wanted it. But he just held the mirror for me. A mirror that was enhanced a million times by the strength of our connection. Now that mirror is shattered. This adventure has come to an end. What a relief.

And then my situation really hits me in my face. I am actually quite fucked. I have no money to get a ticket home, not even to buy another night in this hostel. I have just enough to afford a cup of coffee. To hell with it. I put my sandals on and head to my favorite vegan bar. I meet a friend there – a woman I connected with in another vegan bar a few days earlier. *What are the odds?*

She came for the world's biggest jewelry fair. We hug, she tells me about all the gems she found so far, I tell her what just happened. She offers me the hotel room she double-booked by an accident. A miracle. The first in a long chain of miracles. From that moment on, I am completely supported and held by people I've met during my travels in Thailand and India, and my friends back at home to whom I open up about my travels. I find an old credit card I forgot about. I paid it off a long time ago and was supposed to close it, but I never did. The card was accidentally found in my document folder back at home, when I asked a friend to dig up a paper for my tax self-assessment. I use the card to get my ticket back to the UK and to stay three more weeks in India, where I barely spend any money anyway.

I only realize the extent of this story when I start talking to my friends about what happened. I record a WhatsApp message to Kasia, a girlfriend I met in secondary school. She has me on speakerphone in the car, driving. She gets so angry, yelling unimaginable curses; she has to pull over, get out of the car, and breathe. This shows me just how far gone I was. My other friend researches Kirt and finds articles in old newspapers about his bigger cons. He was never convicted, but he surely made a lot of people angry about very large sums of money. Wow. This really makes me doubt the value of my spiritual experience.

Was it all just a con?

Coming back to the UK is more difficult than anticipated. The pillows on my bed, the lamp and chair in my lounge, the pictures on the walls – everything reminds me of Aya before the big bang. The memory of finding my true self is blurred and seems unreal. I'm lost and confused, in the male labyrinth again.

I meet with my friend Bridget, who tells me her guru stories in exchange for mine. She had three.

"Oh my God, is that a thing?"

"There's a lot of sex addicts out there, capable of making their living out of it because of their ability to dress it all up in beautiful, spiritually-awakened gowns."

"Shit."

A decision grows in me to leave Kirt's side of the story. Why did he do it, did he plan it all along, is everything he told me a lie, is everything he did just a fake cheat of a con-man? The list of questions multiplies in direct proportion to time. And none of them serve me. I'll never get my answers, just as I'll never get my money. I know it's a downward spiral. Let's just focus on myself. What really matters is what I take from it. My experience. And what an experience it was!

Coming Home

I meet with the man I had an open night-time relationship with before going to India. He invites me over for dinner he cooked; he is kind, caring, and interested in my adventures. I tell him everything apart from Kirt. That was the deal – he didn't want to know about my other lovers. Not that I had any, not outside of the big bang.

I met Anton just over a year ago at a Black Monday event – statistically proven the most depressing day of the year, with a record number of suicides. The findings of sociology touched somebody working at the local authority, which then developed into a wellbeing fair showcasing charities, organizations, and therapists of all kinds capable of helping people to lift the veil of depression. He was there. A tall, confident, outspoken CEO, supported by a strong female team of therapists giving away free taster treatments. Charismatic, intelligent, kind. His eyes were sad, like a dog without a home. A sad heart that was astray. Deep in my pelvis, I also felt his fire. A little tickle. And a promise. I immediately grew fond of him, so I flirted. Just a bit. Otherwise, not interested and busy, carrying on with my role as a manager for my mental health charity, recruiting volunteers, changing the paradigm about mental health… I made sure he had my number before the end of the day but left without a goodbye.

A few days later, we had a date – a crazy bike ride in picturesque parts of Devon, coffee sweetened by delicious chocolate cake in a cute little café with a view. I held my wet pants under an electric hand dryer in the toilet, wearing my sexy lace underwear and warm socks, where I connected with a beautiful 85-year-old woman. She was most charming in remembering her romantic stories from her youth. I must say, I was completely enjoying myself, including getting my bum wet from the road. He was so confident, and enjoying himself too. He knew what he was doing. I figured he must have had many girls before. There was something about his effortlessness. He definitely knew the game. I judged that faithfulness was probably not his strength. But to hell with it. I had always been in long-term relationships, loyal and monogamous. Time to taste something else for a change. We arrived back at the garage, and as he finished parking his precious machine with too much horsepower, he locked his keys inside. He tried ringing his friend who had a spare set, but no answer. The situation was bad. There was no way in; no windows, no doors to kick open. Just the metal roller shutters and brick walls – a solid barrier. The keys to his car, his home, and work were all there. At first, he got so angry, swearing and kicking. I wasn't sure what to do with myself. It was a little scary. I moved away a little, giving him space. Ten minutes later, I checked on him again. He was on the roof, removing tiles, making an opening just big enough for him to slide in, between the rafters, through the ceiling joists, landing swiftly on his worktable and with his keys. Next, I see his head sticking out through the opening in the roof, a beaming smile, instructions on how to open the shutters with the key he threw over to me. Half an hour later, I'm in his car and the garage looks like nothing ever happened.

Wow! Honestly? This man is unstoppable. He will always find a way and will stop at nothing.

That really impressed me. I never ever stop with things that matter to me the most. How bizarre. It was so sexy too. From that moment on, I was all in! Finally, I'd found someone to play with, a great match!

The nine months that followed this date were saturated with fiery sex. It was wild, honest, and free. We had sex in the evening, then in the middle of the night, because at least one of us was horny and couldn't sleep, and then again in the morning. He liked to leave his cock in my pussy when falling asleep, and I would try not to move a muscle, to keep it in. I joked I would charge him for parking. And when we weren't making love, he would hug me so tight that I couldn't move. I remember having to negotiate leaving the bed to go to the toilet.

I enjoyed it so much. But every time I wanted something more, I was rejected. I wanted to spend the weekend together, go for holidays, go canoeing, go for a walk, have his keys to surprise him with dinner… it was always a no. Still, the space between us was deliciously amazing. We met most evenings after 8pm, not speaking much, just being together passionately with endless cuddles. I learned to read him in our silence. The expressions on his face, the feet that completed the hug, his breath and his hands – they all told me stories of how he was and what he felt. I knew he had found a home in me. Our connection was so beautiful – honest, raw, unfiltered. But it was never released to the stretch of the daylight. Every morning, I would make us coffee in bed and then we would part, separated again until nightfall. Some evenings he didn't invite me in. Sometimes he didn't speak to me for a week or two and I would regret wanting an open relationship. But then we would meet again. Until one day, I left for India.

What I didn't know was that he realized what he had only when he lost it. I was gone for almost four months, and he became aware of just how much he liked me. It changed him.

Now he's all in. And I'm receiving his kindness. Slowly, I allow myself to develop a desire to be together with this man in a genuine, caring, beautiful way. I want a family.

I am ready!

I feel he is just the man to do this with. A man who gives me the freedom to do what I need to do. A man with passion who respects his elders, is hardworking, has a strong brotherhood. A man I love to share the silence with. When he makes love to me, it's absolute. Don't get me wrong, he's not perfect, but I really enjoy his kind of weird, you know? Goes well with my weird. He's a no-bullshit kind of guy – direct without fluffy corners. No diplomacy, no politics. Sometimes it can be hard to take, but I get to see his raw, unrefined, true nature – pure earth and fire. It took me a year to get used to his intensity. Every time he said no – and he said no quite a lot – I had to face my uncertainties, old assumptions about what a relationship should look like, and my strong desire for affection. And one day, my doubts drove me away from him. I went off to chase dragons and fairytales in India. I had to find my enlightenment. So I left him. I made another cycle. Now I know. I love this man unconditionally. I want him to be the father of my child. I want him to tend our campfire. I'm in love with ordinariness – no more chasing peak experiences.

My friend told me yesterday that there's a queue for Mount Everest. He sent me the photo he found in papers. There's the snowy peak with the last bit to go, and on the ridge, a long line of people, one next to another, probably more than a hundred, tied together with ropes, deprived of oxygen, exhausted, excited, waiting for their turn to ascend. This is very symbolic, no? And so funny. They spend so much time preparing, getting the right gear and into the right shape, finding guides, accommodation, flights… I imagine it takes over six months to get ready. Then you go, it's the challenge of a lifetime, top of the world, and… you wait in the queue, just like at Tesco. How do I claim my money back? I'm not happy with the service. Maybe there's a Himalayan customer support – you can call if you don't die on your way. Yeah, a lot of people die, and they say the queue is one of the reasons. Another metaphor, no?

So I had my fair share of peak experiences, especially after India. And I swear this was the last time I went into this loop of finding happiness outside of me, or chasing enlightenment. No more. I am now happy with ordinariness. I can get completely lost in a bird's song. My garden is so overgrown with all the herbs and medicinal plants, cedar trees, roses, all the weeds with flowers so beloved by bees, bumblebees, and butterflies – can't take them out, no way. And with all the hidden little water pools, my garden is a home for many animals, birds in abundance! I put a sun deck chair in one corner of my garden, a hidden little space just out of reach of my neighbor's windows. Then I take my clothes off and bathe in birdsong and sunshine. There's a peak experience for you, right there!

So I truly want ordinariness. I want to weave a nest with a man and I want to create a little life. I decide to buy two gold rings, and I plot a plan to propose. The ring for Anton has a special groove on the inside, making this solid, heavy gold band much more comfortable to wear.

My ring looks like two intertwined ivy twigs with six diamonds nested on it, very fairy-like, and I like the symbolism of ivy – an evergreen plant that attaches itself to the tree and never lets go. I want that quality in our bond. The rings were made by a beautiful Polish artisan who took two weeks to complete this piece of art. I didn't mind the wait – I had all the time in the world.

Wednesday morning shortly after waking up, still soft and warm in bed, we have a little pleasure. Sex is a little bit off at the moment, but we enjoy each other's company, so I'm not making much of it. Maybe he's stressed, maybe something else. I walk barefoot to the kitchen, look up at the sky through the window in the ceiling. Smile. Make coffee for two. Sing a little song while washing two cups. Take them back to bed, happy to be back in soft cushions. He takes his cup, sits up, and taking his first sip, he asks:

"Have you slept with someone in India?"

Wow, that's a rather big question.

One year ago, when we started seeing each other, we had a brief conversation about having an open relationship. We gave each other permission and neither of us wanted to know the details. I often wondered how many women he slept with, being so masculine, confident, and cocky, his sexual energy coming through in such a visible way – something that women can sense and go for, I'm sure. Many times, I questioned myself for deciding to have this open relationship. I had many nightmares that led to a crisis. But I had conquered this. All the fears about my beauty, aging, needing him exclusively for myself to feel complete and loved… it was so hard at times, but I never quit when it comes to embracing my shadows, so I kept opening and embracing this new phenomenon of being with a man who might be sleeping with others. It really helped me to develop trust in my path with this man completely.

Now he's changing the game. He wants to know.

"I'll tell you everything. Do you really want to know?"

He nods, takes another sip of coffee, then makes himself more comfortable. He's not looking at me. I take a big breath into my belly.

"Yes, one person, I spent six nights with him."

And then, for some reason, I think it's a good idea to add:

"I loved him."

Maybe it would reassure him that I didn't sleep with a man who I didn't love or something. He has another question, his voice calm and slow. He asks if I'm still in contact with him.

"Yes, I left him a message yesterday."

Wow, never before have I been in an open relationship. Never before have I had a conversation like this.

Honestly, I'm doing well at all. Actually, I'm doing really badly. It hurts him on many levels. Looking at him, I suddenly see the softness in him that I've just violently ripped into a thousand pieces. So then I go on saying just how much I love him, that I want a family with him, how I see him as my man, the father of my child. I want to add that it doesn't matter whether I slept with a hundred men in India or just one, I'd still choose him – but I stop myself, because what I see is just so bad. It's in his eyes and his arms. I've hurt him. He is a broken man. He wishes I never existed.

Over the next two weeks, he turns into a deadly wounded bear, roaring, biting, blindly scratching at everything around him. There are words, sentences, tears, anger. I see it, I feel it. I'm so connected to this man. My heart is broken too. At the same time, I'm aware of the irony of this situation. Just as I decided I'm ready for a family, the big brown grizzly bear says NO, making it impossible to proceed. I feel his pain and my deep sadness for causing this. On some level, I also feel I haven't done anything wrong:

Hey, come on, the two of you indulging in this big drama with lots of self-pity. We had an agreement, no? He agreed to this, I had the freedom, though I never actually used it until I found my guru in India. I thought sex with him was going to transcend me beyond this plain, I chased a dream, yet again, but the story itself had punishment in it for me, come on. I'm thirty-nine, and I finally woke up to consciously and joyfully wanting to have a family, to nourish it inside out, and it appears that my actions completely blew it. Well done, Aya!

After I drop the bombshell in that bed, there's really nothing else to say. I pack my stuff and leave to go back home. On my way there, I have a car crash. Just as I was thinking that I'm handling this so well. Honestly, right at that moment, I'm thinking to myself:

Yes, very well, it's a shitty situation, but you're aware, compassionate, present with all the different feelings and thoughts, a prominent Zen student…

Boom! Right, I don't think I'm handling anything at all.

I get out. My car is badly scratched and I'm responsible for the other car's bodywork.

Fuck!

And then it all lands in my body. I get paralysis on the left side of my body. A lot of pain too. Can't move my leg. I limp back to my car. Things are really bad.

How did I end up in this mess?

I need time out.

What's going on?

The owner of the other car is calling someone.

The police? An ambulance?

I don't know.

My ears are buzzing. I realize that I completely blanked him, can't even remember if he was talking to me.

Is he angry?

I don't know.

I dive deep into the stiffness of my hip, knee, and ankle. I feel the pain spreading alongside the body, holding me prisoner, immobile in an invisible plaster cast. I allow myself to go deeper into this immobility.

Yes, make her stop.

Embodying the symptom, I'm becoming the cause of the pain. I'm shapeshifting from being the victim of the pain to being the immobilizing force, the plaster cast, the perpetrator.

No love, you will not move! You shall not progress – not in your relationship, not at work, not with your finances or your understanding of spirituality and shamanism. No discussion. It's a no! Whatever you try, whatever you do – it's always going to be a no!

Aw, hello there. That's the bigger picture. It's no longer just about Anton and my infidelity. There are bigger forces at stake. What an authority, what power! The power to put a glass ceiling on literally every aspect of my life at this moment.

No! You will not pass this point. There's no going beyond this point.

I am creating this. My mind, my thoughts. Nobody else. Nothing else. No system, no situation, no person – me! That's how powerful I am. That's how powerful you are too – would you believe it?

Of course I was never meant to have a family with Anton. I created that desire when I was deeply lost and confused, finding my way through the male labyrinth. It would have been a dead end. But I didn't know. After two months of being an angry bear, Anton found solace in another woman. And the pattern repeated itself. Just as Kirt was unable to leave Dolina to give me what I wanted, now Anton, the unstoppable man, was stuck with his ego-death-sentence, refusing to go to the gallows, escaping with a woman instead. And who could blame him?

It took me another six months to see it. Lots of tears, lots of pain. But finally, I found a way to let him go.

I prayed this morning with tobacco in my garden and I was met by the violent weather of wind and rain. The weather is helping me to change my perspective.

From the moment you took me on the first bike ride, I saw your wild nature – strong, unstoppable, madly in love with the excitement of being alive. And I fell in love with what I saw. I knew you didn't want me, but I loved you anyway. It broke my heart many times over that first year, when all you wanted was to meet for the night. Just a night. But what a night! Passion, endless cuddles, fire, and a safe nest to rest in.

So I kept welcoming the little gifts you had for me and worked hard on eliminating my need for more. I was patient. I didn't show you myself fully, fearing you wouldn't like what I was, so I reined my quirky, fun-loving, adventurous side in.

Deep in my heart, I hoped you would open up to me one day. And in the meantime, I was just giving you love. Unconditionally. Complete acceptance for who you were. And more love. I was open and present for you and took you in completely and fully.

And when I accidentally broke your heart because of the misunderstanding we had, it devastated me. I was broken in half. One half realized that you never took me seriously. Your inability to forgive me was so painful to see – didn't I give you all but love the whole time? Wasn't I always there for you, coming almost every night to your apartment, making love, never complaining about anything, never demanding anything of you? How could this not count? How could you not see my kindness and love?

But the love for you was deep in my bones. So I gifted it to you, in kindness. Taking your anger, taking your sorrow, holding space for the endless sea of your pain.

Then you met someone. Oh, that was painful. A prolonged crucifixion. A betrayal and condemnation. Every night I fell asleep wanting to be in your arms, knowing that you were sleeping with another. But at least you weren't in pain anymore. That brought me solace.

All this love that I gave you the whole time, almost two

years now. My acceptance, my presence, my kindness. It was a gift. You received it well and now you're giving it to Mia. Probably the most challenging thing I have to accept. You're giving her all that I dreamed to receive from you. A family. Building a dream together. Enjoying life together.

And not with me.

All I can do now is accept that I brought this gift of love into your life. I gave it to you, you opened up slowly to receive it, you took what you could, and you're free to do with it whatever you want.

And what you want is to share it with someone else.

The sky is crying today and the wind brings a change.

I can see now that being so stubborn to love you, Anton, despite you not wanting me – I needed to experience this rejection over and over. It has pushed me to unravel a secret; the hidden wound of the little girl who wasn't received by her father. The little Aya was too much for him. And he didn't know how to cope. He didn't have the courage or the heart to be curious about her, to see and appreciate her growth, to let himself get carried away by her uniqueness. It wasn't in his repertoire to show affection or love. And in her little mind, the little Aya felt that if only she was beautiful, smart, better in every way, he would love her. If only she was better. But she knew she was ugly in and out. Dumb. Unworthy in every way. And she grew up in deep shame. It was so hard, and slowly, she pushed the shame deep into the abyss of the unconscious mind. And it ruled her world. She didn't know, but everything she did in her life stemmed from that root. She had to try hard – with her friends, partners, lovers, in her job, yoga, dance, creativity… even in her shamanic practice. She was always not enough. She couldn't know that no matter how hard she tried, she would never win with herself, she would always be unworthy because her dad never appreciated her.

This is not to say I'm a poor little victim of my bad-ass villain father. On the contrary. I am deeply grateful to him also. Thanks to the seed he planted, I had the unwavering intention to keep going, even in times of great suffering, confusion, and no hope. This seed was a necessary tool that brought me to uncover the greatest truth of all. And it served its purpose. I can let go of it now.

So you see, to unearth this, is the greatest gift of all.

My deepest gratitude to you.

My ship is setting sail now, and the winds are strong.

I wish you well.

Aya

I send it to Anton. And then I write another letter, to myself.

My sweet, lovely Aya,

You have been trying so hard. Healing and embracing the totality of human experience. Relentlessly going, hit by the waves of the merciless mind. Most of your experience is showing you just how much resistance you have to stop fully.

You can rest now.

You know the truth. Be present. Be love. Effortlessly.

Allow the light from the heart and the light from the womb to shine on everything around. You are the silver swan. You just need to allow it to be. Rest in your power. Stop resisting. Stop clinging to the cleverly designed visions of adventures that really only bring you lessons to let go and surrender to who you really are.

Feelings are sometimes so hard to experience and so confusing to understand. I know it has been a wild ride for you. I'm deeply grateful for all that's happened. Nothing has to happen next. Just be. In the home of your heart. In the wisdom of your womb. The divine feminine has awakened within you. There is no more hard work. Just allowing everything to be. In kindness.

I love you very much.

Aya

Epilogue

In the months after my realization, I focus on therapeutic work with sound. I make myself available and within the space of nine months, I deliver sound baths to one thousand people. They say how transformational it was, that they feel touched. Eighty women ask me for a private session, and these happen to be initiations into their power. They're not rituals that I pre-plan and deliver from a menu. They happen in the unfolding of the truth between two open bodies, minds, hearts, and wombs. The initiations reignite the connection with forgotten land within. With intuition and source.

All I do is allow myself to stand in the unknown. Trusting and surrendering, open and present. I take a breath in and it happens. It flows from the Earth, from the stars, from within. Some women don't have a womb within their bodies, but they are always able to identify it. Find it. Make a choice to connect with it. Some men feel the feminine strongly in their structure. All in all. The power is ours to claim, to rest in it and as it, to create a new human paradigm with it.